RECLAIMING THE BIBLE
FOR THE CHURCH

RECLAIMING
the
BIBLE
for the
CHURCH

Edited by

CARL E. BRAATEN

and

ROBERT W. JENSON

WILLIAM B. EERDMANS PUBLISHING COMPANY
GRAND RAPIDS, MICHIGAN / CAMBRIDGE, U.K.

Library of Congress Cataloging-in-Publication Data

Reclaiming the Bible for the church /
edited by Carl E. Braaten and Robert W. Jenson.
p.   cm.
"Chapters of this book originated as addresses delivered at a theological
conference on the theme, 'Reclaiming the Bible for the Church,' held at
St. Olaf College in Northfield, Minnesota, June 6-8, 1994" — P. ix.
ISBN 0-8028-0898-0 (pbk.: alk. paper)
1. Bible — Evidences, authority, etc. — Congresses. 2. Bible — Theology —
Congresses. 3. Bible — Canon — Congresses. 4. Bible — Hermeneutics —
Congresses. 5. Bible — Criticism, interpretation, etc. — Congresses.
I. Braaten, Carl E., 1929- . II. Jenson, Robert W.
BS480.R43 1995
220.1'3 — dc20   95-33984
CIP

On behalf of the Center for Catholic and Evangelical Theology, the editors
acknowledge with gratitude a grant in the amount of $5,000 from the Lilly
Endowment Foundation to support a theological conference on "Reclaiming
the Bible for the Church," which was held June 6-8, 1994, at St. Olaf College,
Northfield, Minnesota.

Unless otherwise noted, Scripture quotations are from the New Revised
Standard Version of the Bible, copyright © 1989 by the Division of Christian
Education of the National Council of the Churches of Christ in the U.S.A.,
and used by permission.

Contents

v

CONTENTS

Contributors

ELIZABETH ACHTEMEIER, Adjunct Professor of Bible and Homiletics, Union Theological Seminary, Richmond, Virginia

CARL E. BRAATEN, Director, Center for Catholic and Evangelical Theology, Northfield, Minnesota

BREVARD S. CHILDS, Sterling Professor of Divinity, Yale University, New Haven, Connecticut

KARL P. DONFRIED, Professor of Religion and Biblical Literature, Smith College, Northampton, Massachusetts

ROY A. HARRISVILLE, Emeritus Professor of New Testament, Luther Northwestern Theological Seminary, St. Paul, Minnesota

THOMAS HOPKO, Professor of Theology and Dean, St. Vladimir's Orthodox Theological Seminary, Crestwood, New York

ROBERT W. JENSON, Professor of Religion, St. Olaf College, Northfield, Minnesota

AIDAN J. KAVANAGH, Professor of Liturgics, Yale Divinity School, New Haven, Connecticut

ALISTER E. McGRATH, Professor of Theology, Wycliffe Hall, Oxford, and Regent College, Vancouver, British Columbia

Introduction: Gospel, Church, and Scripture

CARL E. BRAATEN
AND ROBERT W. JENSON

The chapters of this book originated as addresses delivered
at a theological conference on the theme, "Reclaiming the
Bible for the Church." The conference was cosponsored by the
Center for Catholic and Evangelical Theology and the American Lutheran Publicity Bureau and took place in Northfield,
Minnesota, June 6-8, 1994. An ecumenical group of theologians
spoke on the crisis of biblical authority and interpretation in
the church. This preface will introduce some recurrent themes
of the various addresses.

Most of the speakers addressed the gap between the historical-critical method of biblical studies and the church's dogmatic interpretation of biblical faith. The historical-critical
method was originally devised and welcomed as the great
emancipator of the Bible from ecclesiastical dogma and blind
faith. Some practitioners of the method now sense that the
Bible may have meanwhile become its victim. Questions of
every conceivable kind have been put to the biblical texts, but
for many in the church — pastors, teachers, and laity — the
Bible seems to have lost its voice. Can the Bible still speak to
the church in an age of critical historical awareness? Or better,

does God continue to speak his Word through the Bible as a whole?

The image of "reclaiming the Bible" suggests that it has been forsaken or lost. Of course, that is not literally true. There are more Bibles than ever before, and in more languages, dialects, translations, and versions. What needs to be reclaimed for the church is the Bible as authoritative Scripture. There is loss of confidence in the ability of the church to read the Bible through the eyes of its own faith and in light of its own exegetical and liturgical traditions. Is there an ecclesial hermeneutic nonreducible to methods of historical criticism that can be practiced outside the church and apart from faith?

Biblical fundamentalism rejects the use of the historical-critical method *tout court*. There is no hint of that among the authors of this book. Some are front-ranking biblical scholars fully versed in the arts of literary and historical criticism of which their publications demonstrate uninhibited use. But the question is: Does the historical-critical method of biblical interpretation suffice of itself apart from the gospel and the church as the community in which the Bible functions as canon and through which the living voice of God is heard?

The historical-critical method was a gift to the church of the Enlightenment. At first the historical approach was rejected by the theologians of Protestant Orthodoxy and Pietism, but then it gradually gained acceptance among mediating theologians who attempted to reconcile the traditional faith of the church with principles of modern reason. However, the marriage between scholarly criticism of the Bible as a collection of ancient documents and the church's belief in its divinely inspired message of salvation has ever since proved to be unstable. The methods of critical reason have tended to take over the entire operation of biblical interpretation, marginalizing the faith of the church and dissolving the unity of the Bible as a whole into a multiplicity of unrelated fragments. The academy has replaced the church as the home of biblical interpretation. Biblical critics frequently claim that their use of the historical-critical method is free of confessional assumptions and theological motivations, that their approach enjoys the status of objective historical science. Upon close scrutiny, however, it is possible to show that historical critics approach the texts with their own set of prior commitments, sometimes hiddenly linked to ideologies alien or hostile to the faith of the Christian church.

Which hermeneutic, then, is best qualified to understand the Scriptures? That of the autonomous scholar whose private ideological commitment is disguised as objective scientific research or that of a community of faithful memory that forthrightly acknowledges the Scriptures as its divinely inspired authority? Brevard Childs's "canonical method" of biblical interpretation includes the church as intrinsic to a hermeneutic of historical inquiry in search of the true subject matter of the Scriptures. The essayists in this book interact with Childs's canonical approach in an appreciative way, something that can scarcely be said of many in the guild of biblical scholarship who have either ignored his major works or dismissed his approach as too Barthian. But this has become the fate of almost anyone who still treats the Bible as the Word of God and as the canonical source and norm of the church's faith.

Another recurrent theme is that Scripture exists on account of the church and for its sake. Its authority derives from the same gospel that gave birth to the church. The experiences and needs of the church form the appropriate heuristic principles, the *Fragestellung*, for scriptural exegesis. Otherwise what happens is that an alien hermeneutic takes charge of exegesis, and the church is led into heresy or apostasy. Authoritative Scripture functions not as an isolated text in separation from the church, but only in conjunction with the gifts of the Spirit in the life of the church, its apostolic confession of faith and its life-giving sacraments of baptism, absolution, and the Lord's Supper.

The church uses Scripture in its ministry of Word and sacraments to bring people into fellowship with its Author. The Author of Scripture is the Triune God, Father, Son, and Holy Spirit. The trinitarian paradigm in biblical interpretation was a prominent feature of the addresses, worship services, and conversations at the conference on reclaiming the Bible for the church. The *doctrine* of the Trinity is rooted in the gospel of the crucified and risen Lord, Jesus the Christ. The biblical narrative culminates in the gospel's identification of God in the entire story of Jesus' life, death, and resurrection.

In Western theology of the Trinity the Holy Spirit usually comes up short. The concern for a full-fledged doctrine of the Spirit is another recurrent theme in the essays that follow. Western trinitarian theology has often given way to a unitarianism of either the first or second article of the Creed. When the Holy Spirit who is the unity of the Father and the Son drops out of sight, Christian theology self-destructs into deism or "Jesus hero-worship." Without the activity of the Spirit the hermeneutical chain that links us with the mystery of divine salvation in the Word made flesh is broken. Without the Spirit the Bible is just a book of ancient texts and not the canon of holy Scripture. Without the Spirit the gospel is only a myth invented by the friends of Jesus to keep a good thing going. Without the Spirit the church is merely an association of like-minded people who gather from time to time to share religious experiences. Without the Spirit the sacraments are mere aids to remember what happened once upon a time. Thus the Holy Spirit is the great communicator, the sine qua non of reclaiming the Bible for the church as canonical Scripture and of recovering true authority in the church.

On Reclaiming the Bible for Christian Theology

BREVARD S. CHILDS

Some months ago I was invited to write a *Festschrift* essay for a German colleague. In order to address an area of his greatest interest I chose the topic: "The Old Testament in Germany 1920-1940. A Search for a New Theological Paradigm." Only after I had finished the article did I realize some of the broader theological implications for today's struggle over the Bible.

Lessons from a Former Generation's Struggle

The new theological debate in Germany during the 1920s arose in the context of a well-developed, scientific biblical discipline that was confident that any changes that might occur in the future would have to be based on the established historical-critical results of the nineteenth century. The new and unexpected element in the situation was the sudden call by a minority voice for a radical change in direction and for a theological exegesis that would do justice to the Bible's confessional content. Among this group there was a wide-spread agreement that biblical studies had lost their way just

1

when the historical-critical method had won full hegemony in the field.

Of course it was evident that the major stimulus for the new call derived from the rebirth, in Germany, of confessional theology that was associated with figures such as Karl Barth and others. In the field of Old Testament studies Wilhelm Vischer's famous — for many, infamous — book *The Witness of the Old Testament to Jesus Christ* (1934) was a lightning rod. The difficult issue was how the change in exegesis was to be achieved. In an important review published in 1935 *(Theologische Blätter)*, Gerhard von Rad, who even in his early thirties was widely regarded as one of the most promising Old Testament theologians of the church, assessed Vischer's book. Von Rad initially agreed with Vischer's call for a new theological approach, and later in life he freely admitted that Vischer had indeed sounded the alarm, especially in the light of the threat from National Socialism after 1933. However, in his review he attacked Vischer as harshly as any of Vischer's liberal detractors, and concluded that his exegetical approach was quite hopeless. Moreover, it was significant that von Rad did not really attack him theologically, but from the perspective of the historical-critical method. Vischer had not done justice either to form-critical distinctions or to the text's traditio-historical development, but he had fallen back into traditional dogmatic categories. To be sure, von Rad differed from the older critics by substituting his own form of historical-critical exegesis, which built on the work of Alt and Noth and which he offered as a fresh way out of the theological crisis.

However, what was surprising for me was to discover that the radical voice of theological dissent from the 1920s and 1930s had, by 1940, already been considerably domesticated and that a widespread consensus in regard to the Old Testament had formed among German-speaking, confessionally oriented scholars (for example, von Rad, Eichrodt, Zimmerli, and others). It included a highly nuanced position that at the outset unreservedly affirmed the full legitimacy of the historical-critical method. It then sought to preserve the unity of the

Old and New Testaments with some form of *Heilsgeschichte* that rejected the abstraction of philosophical categories and even allowed for differing levels of figurative meaning just as long as the literal sense was not impaired. There was even an attempt to address the concerns of the earlier "pneumatic exegesis" that would recognize the subjective side of faith which Scripture evoked. This widespread Old Testament consensus then resurfaced full blown in the post–World War II era and dominated the German scene for over two decades. Of course, not everyone agreed and voices of opposition from both the left and the right continued to sound, but their influence was minor during this period. Especially impressive in the postwar era was that the two theologies of von Rad and Bultmann seemed to be able to combine a rigorous historical-critical approach together with a deep existential concern for Christian theology.

It is now clear in hindsight that both these theologies began to experience serious erosion by the late 1960s, and the widening cracks signaled the breaking apart of the biblical consensus. It lies beyond the scope of our present concerns to pursue the reasons why the post–World War II biblical consensus in Germany began to deteriorate so rapidly. Of the several complicated factors involved, a few appear clear.

1. Many of the critical hypotheses of Alt, Noth, and von Rad dissolved under closer scrutiny.

2. The theological climate of the postwar period began to change and the existential kerygmatic language of the *Kirchenkampf* shared by von Rad and Bultmann appeared increasingly alien to a new generation.

3. German church and culture along with the rest of the West became increasingly secularized and a new political, cultural, and personal agenda turned attention away from theological concerns that still had deep traditional and ecclesial roots.

4. Finally, with the passing of the generation that had been tested in the crucible of the tumultuous 1930s, no one of the stature of Barth, Bultmann, and von Rad arose to take their place, and theology entered a quieter and less exciting era.

3

Perhaps one of the most important implications to be drawn from this history of German scholarship lies in the observation that many of the hermeneutical issues that evoked such controversies in the 1920s and 1930s still remain unresolved, and, with the erosion of the post–World War II consensus, have returned with a vengeance. Yet the issues of today have arisen in a strikingly different, pluralistic, and secular context. The primary struggle no longer is how to relate traditional faith with modern scientific methodology, nor is there a strong voice from the side of dogmatic theology calling biblical studies back to confessional roots; rather, the direction has been the reverse. In the English-speaking world especially, the challenge stems from those biblical scholars who question modern theology's attempt to reflect theologically without any serious appeal to Scripture.

The issue of major debate at present being carried on largely within a secular university context is not whether there is a legitimate theological exegesis, but whether the Bible in any form can be anything more than an expression of time-conditioned human culture. Or again, the modern debate is not over the right of a literal or figurative sense of Scripture to bear witness to Jesus Christ, but over whether any ancient text has a determinate meaning, and whether interpretation is simply an exercise in ever-changing modes of deconstruction. Finally, the issue is whether the Scriptures can serve as a guide to faithful living, a position that has been challenged by those who recognize only sociological forces at work at a time when various Christian communities are seeking to establish their identities with warrants from the past.

As a young scholar along with many confessing Christians I too felt the full force of the powerful challenge of Barth, Vischer, and Hellbardt for the Old Testament to be heard as a theological witness to Christian faith. Yet I was also forced to agree with von Rad, Eichrodt, and Zimmerli that Vischer's solution was seriously flawed and that there must be an alternative to the sharp polarity that he set up between modern historical-critical exegesis and a repristination of sixteenth-century Reformation theology.

4

The painful lesson that has emerged in the last fifty years is that the many serious attempts at a theological compromise that would build a confessional biblical theology directly on the foundation of a historical-critical method (Eichrodt, von Rad, Zimmerli, Bultmann, Jeremias, Stuhlmacher, Küng) have also failed, at least as measured by the theological call of the 1930s. The gap between critical biblical studies and Christian theology is as great as in the pre-1920 era. Whatever the weaknesses were in the debate of the 1920s and 1930s, it remains the enduring contribution of Barth, Vischer, and Hellbardt, among others, rightly to have insisted that the living, unfettered voice of God in Scripture cannot be held captive to the norms of human rationality.

What then is to be the direction for the church as it moves toward reclaiming the Bible for its theological reflection? It would be the height of folly and sheer arrogance to suggest that the issue can be resolved simply by an appeal to "canonical criticism." The issues are far too complex and lie too deep to be resolved by a few techniques or clever proposals. However, I would argue that the issues encompassed within the cipher "canon," namely, Scripture, church, Word, and Spirit, address those basic theological factors — strangely missing in many of the previous debates — without which no truly theological solution to reconcile the church's Scriptures with modernity can ever be reached.

Let me then try to expand on this statement and draw out some of the theological implications at stake.

Theological Role of Historical Criticism of the Bible

Historical research over the last two hundred years has demonstrated in a fully convincing way that the relation between the written form of the Bible and its authorship is a highly complex one. Yet it is right at this juncture that traditional conservative Christianity has balked. These scholars have argued that unless the Bible is historically correct in its ascription of direct authorship to Moses, to Isaiah, to Paul and Peter, its theological credibility is seriously called into question. Therefore, conservatives have concentrated their apologetic in defending as far as possible the Mosaic authorship of the Pentateuch, the unity of Isaiah, the Johannine authorship of the fourth Gospel, and Paul's writing of the Pastorals. Critics like James Barr, of course, have a field day in pointing out the inconsistency in much of this endeavor.

The problem is that Barr and all the defenders of the Enlightenment have never grasped the true nature of the hermeneutical issues at stake. Rather, one has to give credit to the work of scholars such as Kähler, Schlatter, Barth, and many others, who at least have pointed in a new direction for serious hermeneutical reflection. Among modern Catholic biblical scholars great exegetical illumination has been provided, for example, by Schürmann, Schelkle, and Vögtle, who have sought to combine in a profoundly theological fashion traditional Catholic learning and historical-critical reflection. In more recent times the canonical approach has tried to resist the inherent rationalism of the traditional conservative position — it stems ultimately from the assumptions of natural theology — when it applies modern categories of authorship to ancient Scripture. Rather, it has sought to understand and interpret the Bible's own categories within its larger context and to pursue the theological function that such categories serve. For example, we all know the literary and historical problems associated with the Mosaic authorship of the Pentateuch, and how conservatives struggled to reconcile their affirmation of direct authorship with Deuteronomy's account of Moses' death. Nevertheless it is very important theologically that the role of Moses as the divinely appointed tradent of the law not be dismissed out-of-hand, a persistent error of liberal critical scholarship. It is fully clear that the editors of the Old Testament — the canonical shapers in my terminology — operated from a different perspective when they argued in a circle. If a law was authoritative for Israel, it must be from

6

Moses. Conversely, if Moses was its divine source, then it must be authoritative for Israel.

My revered teacher, Judah Goldin, used to speak in his midrash seminar at Yale of "Jewish logic." He would announce in a highly provocative tone: "I can prove to you from the Bible that Moses always wore a yarmulka, that is, a hat. Does not Exodus 18 say that Moses 'went out to meet his father-in-law'? But when does an observant Jew ever go outside without a hat? Thus it is obvious that Moses always wore a hat when he was in the open." Even this silly parody clearly reflects a different attitude toward Scripture and authority from that shared by the rationalists both on the left and right of the theological spectrum.

May I pursue this issue one step further? During the spring semester I taught an English exegesis of the book of Isaiah as Christian Scripture. I spent considerable time tracing the different levels of material within the Isaianic corpus and in tracing the history of the book's composition, which as you know is a highly complex problem. After about six weeks one conservative student raised an objection. He asked: "Why go through all these scholarly contortions? Why not take the word of Isaiah's superscription literally: This is 'the vision of Isaiah.' God gave the prophet a divine unveiling of the future that could encompass the Assyrian, Babylonian, and Persian periods without a problem."

I found myself responding as if by reflex with the familiar historical-critical response:

We now know that the Old Testament prophets were not foretellers, but "forthtellers" (G. A. Smith).

Prophets addressed a concrete historical community of Israelites with political, social, and religious issues commensurate with their historical milieu rather than dealing with issues of the distant future.

Finally, the prophetic literature is such that to construe the word "vision" as a form of supernatural clairvoyance does not do justice to the complex shape of the material, which reflects different genres, a great variety of historical settings, and complex problems of editorial shaping that took years to accomplish.

Later, after further reflection, I realized that I had not done justice to the theological dimensions of the question. In this regard, the historical-critical response was sorely deficient and the lack was acutely felt by the student, even when ineptly expressed. I do not deny the important elements of truth in the critical response, but it is theologically inadequate. Indeed, right at this point one can glimpse the fresh impact of the canonical approach.

The traditions of Isaiah have been textualized and transmitted in written form as a book to serve as authoritative Scripture for later generations of Israel. This process of the transformation of function was already adumbrated in chapter 8 when the prophet Isaiah assigned his earlier oracles, which had been rejected during the Syrian-Ephraimic war, to his disciples for transmission and reuse by a later generation. In a word, Isaiah's original oracles have undergone a change of function. Isaiah's role as a prophet can no longer be described as that of an eighth-century "forthteller," but in textualized form his words now serve as an authoritative foretelling, a prophetic vision to later generations of Israel for whom the word is still a divine commission. Moreover, the earlier oracles have been retained in all their fragmentary and broken form, but his words have received a new role. It is therefore crucial that biblical exegesis not be just a reconstruction of some theoretical original form in the life of the prophet. Rather, an important part of exegesis is to deal theologically with the canonical shape of the tradition, which has been holistically rendered as a divine revelation embracing the future. Quite obviously this is the manner in which 1 Peter 1:10f. understood the role of the Old Testament prophet:

> The prophets who prophesied of the grace which was to be yours searched and inquired about this salvation; they inquired what person or time was indicated by the spirit of Christ within them when predicting the sufferings of Christ and the subsequent glory. (RSV)

8

In one sense, the canonical approach recognizes the need of a "second naiveté" (Ricoeur) to acknowledge the complexity of the shaping of Scripture, and yet also to see the Bible from a different and unified perspective: that of the community of faith who bore witness by its transmission to the continuing redemptive intervention of the one divine reality, whom the church confesses to be the God and Father of Jesus Christ. Unless such a theological move is attempted by the biblical interpreter, it is difficult to see how the bridge to a modern theological reflection within the context of the Christian faith can be successfully made. Of course the canonical warrant for the move lies in the conviction that Scripture itself has been shaped by this very openness to the future generations of faith and to an anticipation of the eschatological in-breaking of God's reign.

The Relation of Canon to the Community of Faith

The terms "canon" and "Scripture" are very closely related, indeed often identical. Yet to speak of canon in the context of a community of faith is to bring out the special nuance of the term "canon," namely, that the authoritative writings of the church were transmitted and received in response by a faithful people of God. These writings did not fall unmediated from heaven. Canon lays stress on the process of receiving and transmitting the treasured oracles of God. Moreover, this process of reception was not that of the recipients serving a passive role as an inert conduit, but as living and active tradents who both selected, formed, and ordered the Scriptures toward the goal of engendering faith and instructing every successive generation in righteousness. The church has always confessed a faithful transmission of the gospel (contra Reimarus). God has not left the church without a truthful witness to himself as testified to by the prophets and the apostles.

The issue of canon and community of faith touches on the old theological battle between Protestants and Catholics

9

that fell under the rubric of "word and tradition." These two components were split apart during the heated debates of the sixteenth century. The Catholics insisted on the primacy of church tradition in forming the Bible; the Protestants argued for the primacy of the Word as the ultimate source of Scripture. However, I suspect that among modern theologians of both camps there is widespread agreement that these two components belong indissolubly together, as had once been so eloquently defended by Irenaeus. Scripture does not bring forth a witness to itself, but points to God's Word calling the church into existence. Yet the community of faith actively received, shaped, and transmitted the Scriptures and the church provides the context for its correct interpretation for faith and practice. This means that proper interpretation does not consist of an initial stance of seeking a purely objective or neutral reading to which the element of faith is added subsequently, but rather, from the start, the Christian reader receives a particular point of standing from which to identify with the apostolic faith in awaiting a fresh word from God through the Spirit.

I would also argue that the editors shaped the biblical material throughout the various levels of its transmission by means of signs, signals, and structural features so that the reader could be guided in construing Scripture canonically, that is, kerygmatically. Two examples, one from the Old and one from the New Testament, serve to illustrate the argument.

The literary composition of the book of Deuteronomy is generally assigned by critical research to the seventh century and is historically related in some fashion to the reforming of Judah's cult by King Josiah. Yet in its present place within the Pentateuch, it has been given a new and particular canonical role. It now functions to provide a hermeneutical guide on how law in Exodus, Numbers, and Leviticus is to be interpreted theologically. Moses is portrayed as explaining the divine will to a new generation that has itself not experienced the events of exodus and the entering into a covenant with God at Sinai. Moses instructs the people who stand poised on the edge of the promised land on how to apply the law as a "rule of faith" for their new life. God's covenant is not tied to the past generation, but it is still offered to "all of us here alive this day" (5:3); therefore, "walk in all the way which the LORD your God has commanded you, that you may live" (v. 33, RSV). Indeed, all the prior law can be summarized in terms of loving God, heart, soul, and might (6:5). The very fact that Old Testament law can be summarized provides a major check against all forms of legalism, which misunderstands the will of a living God for his people.

Luke's Gospel was originally part of a two-volume work that was integrally connected with the Acts of the Apostles. Yet the canonical role of Luke's Gospel has been altered in such a way as to provide it with a new function within the larger New Testament corpus. Luke's first volume has been separated from the second volume of Acts and assigned as an independent work to the collection of the other Gospels, which now forms the context for its interpretation. In short, Luke's witness to Christ has been canonically ordered according to its subject matter, which it has in common with the other Gospels. His Gospel is not to be interpreted as the personal ideology of some Greco-Roman author, but rather as another authoritative testimony to the one gospel, the witness to which it shares with the fourfold canonical corpus even while remaining uniquely "the Gospel . . . according to Luke." Of course, the exact relationship among the four is never spelled out in the New Testament other than that of their being united in bearing witness to the one gospel. The task of exegesis according to this model is therefore to pursue the nature of this unity and diversity in terms of the common subject matter that is God's good news and that serves as an overarching *regula fidei*.

The Relation of the Two Testaments

One of the most difficult but crucial questions for any attempt at reclaiming the Bible for Christian theology turns on the way

11

by which one understands the relation between the two Testaments. The Christian church is unanimous in affirming that its Scriptures consist of two parts, an Old and a New Testament. The church made the boldest possible move in laying claim to the Jewish Scriptures as part of its own canon. For two centuries the early church had only the Scriptures of the synagogue for its own normative writings. It continued to receive them as authoritative, and it joined them to its evangelical traditions both in written and oral form. Moreover, it is crucial to understand that the church did not adopt the Jewish Scriptures as merely background to the New Testament, but it made the theological claim that the Jewish Scriptures, that is, the Old or Former Testament, bore witness to Jesus Christ.

However, apart from this affirmation of the canonical role of both the Old and New Testaments, the exact relationship between the two was never spelled out in any creed. Rather, various theologians of the church continued to struggle with the issue, usually reacting strongly against usages (by Marcion, the Gnostics, and the Ebionites) that appeared to do injury either to God or Christ, and were thereby deemed heretical. Several classic rubrics emerged as most characteristic of the church's handling of the problems of prophecy and fulfillment, progressive revelation, and law and gospel. One of the most familiar moves in resolving these problems, which became virtually a reflex in the early and medieval periods, was a highly developed form of figurative or allegorical reading. The chief disadvantage was that, increasingly, the semantic level of the Old Testament was altered, which allowed the text to be easily harmonized with the New Testament.

Right from the inception of the church a powerful force was exerted by Jewish scholars who offered another and often very different interpretation of the Old Testament texts from that of the Christian scholars. This exegesis became particularly challenging when French Jewish scholars in the eleventh and twelfth centuries (for example, Rashi) argued hermeneutically for the "plain sense" of the text, which although a highly nuanced rendering, served as a call to interpret the Bible contextually rather than allowing the free imaginative construals of traditional midrash or allegory. With the rise of the modern historical-critical approach the problem for interpreting both Testaments — especially the Old — was greatly intensified. Indeed, the Enlightenment's insistence that an interpretation do justice to the literal or historical sense of the Bible caused the church seriously to rethink its interpretive approach.

The new methods developed by scholars in the wake of the Enlightenment became the source for both great opportunity and serious threat, a tension that remains up to the present. In terms of theology one of the first and disastrous effects was separating the Old from the New Testament and interpreting each solely in terms of its own historical milieu. It became a truism that the New Testament had been influenced by the Old, but that the Old Testament could in any way be interpreted by the New — recall Augustine's famous formulation — was an idea dismissed as hopelessly anachronistic. As a result, for well over 150 years critical scholarship has sought to interpret the Old Testament on its own historical and linguistic terms, albeit with the appeal to such philosophical concepts as eternal truths, or according to an evolutionary scheme of development, in order to maintain at least some loose connection between the two Testaments.

At this juncture the contribution of a canonical approach can be clearly seen. This approach initially agrees with the Enlightenment in affirming that the Old Testament should be understood in its own right. Nevertheless, it interprets this move in a very different manner. The Old Testament is to be understood in its own right because it has its own Jewish voice, which was never altered by the coming of Jesus Christ. Indeed, it was this very Jewish voice that bore witness to the gospel. The crucial factor in a canonical approach lies in recognizing that the concept of the Old Testament's own right has dramatically been altered because of its new context within the larger Christian Bible. The Old Testament's discrete voice is still to be heard, but in concert with that of the New. The two voices are neither to be fused nor separated, but heard together. The exegetical task thus becomes one of doing justice to the unique sounds of each witness within the context of the entirety of the Christian Scriptures.

It should also be obvious that unless one can reach some clarity on this crucial issue of relating the two Testaments, it is quite impossible to speak of reclaiming the Christian Bible for Christian theology.

Interpreting the Bible in Terms of Its True Subject Matter

Several times in the discussion up to now mention has been made of the need for biblical interpretation to address the subject matter, that is, the reality, the *res* of the Bible. Now it is time to deal more directly with this issue which is crucial to the entire argument. There can be no serious use of the Bible for theology unless one has a clear idea of how the interpreter moves from a description of the biblical witness to the object toward which these witnesses point. Previously I have insisted on biblical theology's doing justice to the discrete voices of the two Testaments, but equally important is the pursuing of these voices to the subject matter of which they speak.

Unfortunately, for many within the biblical guild, to focus one's attention on an alleged theological subject matter is a large step backward that can only result in some form of philosophical abstraction such as a static deposit of truth or a ground-of-being. They raise the obvious objection: Has not the entire history of biblical scholarship since the Enlightenment been a struggle to free the discipline from the restraints of Christian dogmatic theology? In my opinion, this objection entails an unfortunate caricature of the approach being proposed.

Rather, I would agree with David Steinmetz's astute observation (*Theology Today*, 1980) that historical critics share a proclivity to defer the question of truth endlessly. Historical description is not enough, but it belongs to the central task of

14

exegesis to move from the witness to the reality of which Scripture speaks. One of the unfortunate effects of much narrative theology is that it gives the impression that one can only retell the story, but it is precisely Scripture's claim to speak the truth that separates its gospel from that of simply a story. Rather, the goal of the interpretation of Christian Scriptures is to understand both Testaments as witness to the self-same divine reality who is the God and Father of Jesus Christ.

The dialogical move of theological reflection that is being suggested traverses the partial and fragmentary grasp of reality found in both Testaments to the full reality that the church confesses to have found in Jesus Christ. Both Testaments bear witness to the One Lord, in different ways, at different times to different people, and yet both are understood in the light of the living Lord himself, the perfect reflection of the glory of God (Heb. 1). In this sense, true biblical interpretation involves a *Sachkritik*, but one in which the *Sache* is defined in terms of the reality of Jesus Christ.

It may seem to some that the call for biblical exegesis to be aggressively concerned with the theological truth of its witnesses is an encroachment on the field of dogmatic theology. Actually I am not worried when the sharp line that separates biblical studies from dogmatics becomes somewhat blurred. Naturally there should remain a division of labor, but this is a strategic judgment, and not one of principle. Because of the training and interest of biblical scholars, the weight of their contribution will remain largely on describing and interpreting biblical texts. Conversely, systematic theologians bring a variety of well-honed philosophical, theological, and analytical skills to bear that are invaluable in relating the study of the Bible to the subject matter of Christian theology. The ultimate test of the success of the cooperation between the two fields lies in the degree to which the biblical text and its subject matter are illuminated.

BREVARD S. CHILDS

The Theological Role of the History of Interpretation

I would conclude this essay on reclaiming the Bible for Christian theology with a plea to both biblical scholars and theologians for a recovery of the church's exegetical tradition. Often as children of the Enlightenment we continue to assume that nothing of importance exegetically occurred before the nineteenth century. In this regard, the contrast between Barth and Brunner or Bultmann — not even to speak of Tillich — could not have been greater. Barth reckoned with a serious exegetical continuity from the church's inception through the modern era with no assumed superiority given to the latter period. Conversely, Brunner and Bultmann, although occasionally citing a Reformer, accepted the widespread critical hypothesis that the nineteen century had irreparably shattered the church's "pre-critical" interpretation of the Bible. What a travesty to speak of Basil, Augustine, and Thomas as pre-critical!

I would fully agree that one needs special training, indeed an unusual empathy, to be able to overcome the initial sense of strangeness with the exegesis of the Early Fathers and the Medieval Schoolmen. One cannot pose to Chrysostom the questions of Gunkel, nor address Bultmann's problems to Calvin. Equally important is the recognition, sadly misunderstood by traditionalists, that the past cannot be simply repristinated. Our relation to the church's exegetical tradition must be one of analogy. Can we interpret the Bible with the same theological seriousness in our postmodern era as our precursors did in theirs? Then if we have the required skills and empathy, the great Christian exegetes of the past can serve as invaluable guides to the future in countless ways.

First, they have an unswerving concern to direct their interpretation to the subject matter of Scripture, which afforded them a sense of the whole. There is little patience among the Fathers with the *sensus trivialis* because they come to the biblical text to hear the voice of God. Secondly, the church's

16

earlier interpreters had the ability to make crucial theological distinctions within the larger context of Scripture as a "rule of faith," and they struggled to do justice to the ultimate theological coherence of the Scriptures rather than assuming irreconcilable diversity. Finally, these scholars of the church directed their exegesis to a congregation of believers who were assembled in anticipation of a fresh word from God. This accounts for their concern that the Bible not be a word simply from the past, but one that reflects the living voice of God working through the Spirit, and thus speaking existentially to the present condition of need.

The challenge of reclaiming the Bible for the church is awesome, particularly at a time in which the academic guild is moving in exactly the opposite direction. Yet this is hardly the first time in which the church is forced to confess its impotence and once again to lay claim to the promise of the gospel for rebirth and renewal. The way to reclaiming the Scriptures will never be easy, but in a time as critical as ours, can we do less than try?

Alien Hermeneutics and the Misappropriation of Scripture

KARL P. DONFRIED

I. The Bible and the Church: The Problem

The theme of this volume, "Reclaiming the Bible for the Church," suggests that the Bible no longer stands in the service of the church among many of those who claim to be its interpreters. Indeed, what has happened today is a shift in the context in which Scripture is interpreted, a shift from the church to the academy. Further, this social shift has often forged a new alliance with the academy in opposition to the classical expressions of the Christian faith. In the name of history, which often is a pretense for an ideological theology, classical and normative expressions of Christian theology are frequently attacked, at times overtly and at times more invidiously and subtly. One need only think of such recent books as Burton Mack's *The Lost Gospel*,[1] Jan Schaberg's *The Illegitimacy of Jesus*,[2] or *The Five Gospels*[3] pro-

---

1. Burton Mack, *The Lost Gospel: The Book of Q and Christian Origins* (San Francisco: Harper, 1993).

2. Jane Schaberg, *The Illegitimacy of Jesus: A Feminist Theological Interpretation of the Infancy Narratives* (San Francisco: Harper, 1987).

3. Robert W. Funk, Roy W. Hoover, and the Jesus Seminar, *The Five*

19

duced by the Jesus Seminar. With regard to the latter Richard Hays asks: "Does the passive, politically correct, laconic sage who speaks in the red type of *The Five Gospels* have the capacity to remake our imaginative world and provide a new fiction within which millions might find meaning for their lives? Surely not."[4]

To a large degree the distorting effects of this social shift can be observed in a variety of secular interpretations, interpretations that are often removed from the faith and practice of those communities who worship Christ as Lord within a trinitarian theology and ecclesiology. What lies at the core of many of these nontrinitarian hermeneutical[5] enterprises is an epistemological monism that assumes that historical knowledge is omniscient and that it determines theological truth.[6] As a result certain biblical texts are disabled and removed from their synchronic construct; this "disabling" function takes place either through a process of "bracketing" (for example, Eph. 5:20-32)[7] or "fixing" (for example, Rom. 1:26-28). The goal

---

Gospels: The Search for the Authentic Words of Jesus (New York: Macmillan, 1993).

4. Richard B. Hays, "The Corrected Jesus," *First Things* 43 (May 1994): 48.

5. A trinitarian hermeneutic of Scripture understands, together with the church fathers, that Jesus is the definitive revelation of God. His life and ministry is not only a word about God, it is the Word of God incarnate. The continued presence of the risen Jesus through the Spirit in the community that worships him leads to the affirmation of a trinitarian theology as the most adequate manner in which to understand the revelation of Being (e.g., Exod. 3:13) in creation, in the history of Israel, in Jesus, and in the church. God is Trinity precisely because he has revealed himself as Father, Son, and Holy Spirit throughout the history of Israel, Jesus, and the church. See also the discussion in Brevard S. Childs, *Biblical Theology of the Old and New Testaments* (Minneapolis: Fortress, 1993), 521.

6. See the review essay by Luke Timothy Johnson, "The Crisis in Biblical Scholarship," *Commonweal* (December 3, 1993): 18-21, especially p. 20.

7. In *The Lectionary for the Christian People*, ed. Gordon W. Lathrop and Gail Ramshaw-Schmidt, Cycle A and B (Yukon, Okla.: Pueblo Publishing Company, 1986-87), the symbol § is placed before Eph. 5:21-23 (Cycle B,

of this "fixing" is that selected texts are made to become dysfunctional and are thus eliminated from contemporary theological dialogue and discourse. Several prominent New Testament scholars have attempted to disable Romans 1:18-32 precisely in such a way.[8] The sins of the Gentile world that Paul has itemized no longer speak to current discussions of sexuality because the worldview expressed belongs to the Apostle's Jewish-Hellenistic background. Such a perspective, it is maintained, can be discarded since it has been superseded by the "insights" of the social sciences. What emerges here is an appeal to history, the philosophical presuppositions of which are seldom, if ever, discussed, coupled with an invocation of the social sciences; together they become the epistemological keys that arbitrate the appropriateness of classical theological and moral teachings for the contemporary church.

It is precisely this unexamined epistemological monism and uncritical appeal to the social sciences that is largely responsible for the cacophany of diverse and discordant voices that parade themselves under the label of "biblical scholarship." The quest for the "real" Jesus is as alive and well today as it was in the eighteenth and nineteenth centuries. By simply changing the name of some of the characters, Schweitzer's critical analysis of the so-called old quest is as damaging today as it was then.[9] Many in the professional guild of biblical scholarship are satisfied to offer private ideological speculations, yielding a myriad of conflicting options distant from the canonical witness

---

p. 202). This and other similar texts are described as "essentially sexist in speaking specifically of a subordinate position of women. Such problematic lessons are translated faithful to the original, with the hope that future lectionary revisions will choose other readings as more appropriate for today's church. Such lessons are marked with a §" (Cycle A, p. xiv).

8. Arland Hultgren, "Being Faithful to the Scriptures: Romans 1:26-27 as a Case in Point," to be published in a volume sponsored by the Evangelical Lutheran Church in America, 1993; Krister Stendahl in a lecture given to West Coast clergy, Fall 1993.

9. Albert Schweitzer, *The Quest for the Historical Jesus* (London: A. &. C. Black, 1911).

and alien to its major theological testimonies. When Vincent of Lerins argued that the center of the faith is "that which has been believed everywhere, always and by all,"[10] he was referring to a theology that was based on the "rule of faith," apostolic authority, and the canon of Scripture; he did not base it on "the fragile vessel of historiography posing as theology."[11]

What indeed are the criteria of discernment that can be usefully employed at this moment in Christian history to sort out these polyphonic and polyvalent claims, not to mention the supplications being foisted upon the contemporary Christian by virtually every publisher intent to sell the "newest contributions" and "radical breakthroughs" of biblical scholarship?

II. The Bible and the Church: Historical Criticism and the Problem of an Alien Hermeneutic

It has become quite fashionable today, in reaction to the problems just outlined, to assume that the culprit is the so-called historical-critical method. First, one needs to be clear that there is no such thing as *a* historical-critical method; there is a variety of methods and hermeneutics in which various components used in the task of historical biblical criticism — that is, textual criticism, literary criticism, form criticism, redaction criticism, just to cite a few — can be employed, often with strikingly different, if not contradictory, results.[12] It is far more accurate to use the phrase "historical biblical criticism," by which is meant the attempt to understand what the biblical author wished to convey to the audience for which he wrote. Since

10. Vincent of Lerins, "Commonitorium," in Henry Bettenson, *Documents of the Christian Church* (Oxford: Oxford University Press, 1963), 83.

11. Johnson, "Crisis," 20.

12. For an excellent discussion of the function and value of historical biblical criticism, see the report of the Pontifical Biblical Commission, "The Interpretation of the Bible in the Church," *Origins* 23/29 (January 6, 1994): 497-524.

all Christians, especially preachers and theologians, must be subject to the control of the written canonical text, and not to spiritual or ideological speculations unrelated to the text, historical biblical criticism, as thus defined, becomes an indispensable tool. And here it is important to pay tribute to the enormous advances and contributions that have been made by many biblical scholars, especially in this century, toward understanding what the biblical authors intended to communicate to their readers.

In a 1981 publication I asserted that it is impossible to effectively preach or practice theology without first attempting to understand the original audience to which the biblical books were addressed;[13] I continue to maintain this position. It would be naive to think that a modern person can, without effort, understand the intention of authors writing in other languages and with different worldviews some nineteen hundred years ago. While the insights resulting from historical biblical criticism have been significant and some results certain, it must also be admitted that many other historical issues remain unresolved or, at least, uncertain. Nevertheless, it must be affirmed that this critical task remains foundational for the entire theological enterprise.

The issue, then, is not with the tools employed by historical biblical critics — otherwise one would have to put into question the very text of Scripture as well as its translations — but the domain of meaning into which the results of such critical study are placed. The real issue is the hermeneutical context, not the critical task itself. It is this universe of meaning that will determine how the scholarly results are used. A prominent theologian suggested to me some years back that what he witnessed at the national Society of Biblical Literature meetings was an exercise in "foundationless hermeneutics."[14] As suggestive as this analysis is, further reflection cautions that

13. Karl Paul Donfried, *The Dynamic Word: New Testament Insights for Contemporary Christians* (San Francisco: Harper, 1981).
14. In conversation with Professor George Lindbeck.

there really is no such thing as a foundationless or neutral hermeneutic. Many, believing that historical criticism represents such a neutral hermeneutic, fall captive to an imperialism that affirms, skillfully and subtly to be sure, that the historical-critical method, in effect, exhausts the meaning of the biblical text. And then, when "historical" is identified with "purely human," for many, quite unconsciously, the christological and trinitarian context of the canon is dismissed as no longer relevant, if not alien to the task of biblical interpretation.

Let me illustrate how such a process can come about by referring to "The Romans Debate."[15] One important aspect of this dialogue has been to determine the occasion and purpose of Romans. To do so involves knowledge of the Graeco-Roman world, inscriptions, the sociological structure of the Jewish and Christian communities in Rome, form criticism, rhetorical and epistolary theory, just to mention a few of the necessary components of the critical task. The result of this historical inquiry and debate has contributed valuable information and shed new light on the situation of Roman Christianity and, further, has advanced a new consensus concerning the actual situations that Paul may have been addressing in writing this letter. Yet in reviewing the course of the discussion one can observe some troubling trends: (1) a tendency on the part of some scholars toward atomistic fixations and fanciful reconstructions with little basis in fact and to which no critical controls are applied; (2) a tendency to permit issues external to the text (important as they may be in their own right), such as the Jewish-Christian dialogue, to determine the evaluation of the theology of Romans; and (3) a tendency to get mired in historical issues and then not to return to the central question that must confront any serious interpreter of the letter: How does this new knowledge help us in understanding Paul's theological message to the Romans? The final essay by Peter Stuhlmacher in the new edition of *The Romans Debate* is a superb model of how histori-

15. See Karl P. Donfried, *The Romans Debate* (Peabody, Mass.: Hendrickson, 1991).

cal biblical criticism contributes to a more profound understanding of the central theological theme in Romans, namely, the righteousness of God.

As one becomes increasingly aware of the fallacy of playing the game of historical reconstruction for its own sake and thinking that it alone exhausts the meaning of Scripture, we need, however, to be beware of the opposite fallacy, namely, to think that one can resolve this dilemma by reverting to a new kind of biblical literalism. To understand the proper historical setting of the canonical texts is essential, while at the same time recognizing the necessary limits of this information. To reject such a historical approach runs the danger of catering to one of the major delusions of the modern age: a self-authority that argues that the only meaning of a text is what it says to me; I alone am the final determiner of meaning and significance. The trinitarian church has always rejected such an introverted and distorted hermeneutic and must continue to do so today. "What the biblical text said to its first readers," suggests Raymond Brown, "should be related to what the text says to me, because I am a Christian heir to the people of Israel and the people of the early church, and *not independent of them*."[16]

All of these considerations are driving us increasingly toward a fundamental question, namely, what is the nature of Scripture and how does it function within an ecclesiological, trinitarian hermeneutic? How does such a hermeneutic inform us about the Triune God, his relationship to us, and the doing of his will? The issues that need further investigation and consideration can perhaps be best illustrated by reviewing certain hermeneutical approaches that are either ambiguous or alien. Most prominent among these erroneous approaches is the failure to be cognizant of the entire canonical context of Christian Scripture as a narrational and theological whole, that is, from Genesis

---

16. Raymond E. Brown, "The Contribution of Historical Biblical Criticism to Ecumenical Church Discussion," in Richard John Neuhaus, *Biblical Interpretation in Crisis: The Ratzinger Conference on Bible and Church* (Grand Rapids: Eerdmans, 1989), 46 [italics mine].

through Revelation, centered in the trinitarian God who has revealed himself definitively in the death and resurrection of Jesus Christ, and to substitute instead certain alien hermeneutical principles that are abstracted from such a universe of meaning.

Such an alien hermeneutic is central to the study draft entitled "The Church and Human Sexuality: A Lutheran Perspective" and produced by the Evangelical Lutheran Church in America.[17] After citing Rom. 13:8-10, the following observation is made: "This love which does 'no wrong to a neighbor' and fulfills all the commandments is pivotal for evaluating homosexual activity. Through Jesus Christ, the heart of the Law is revealed as love of God and love of neighbor. Gay and lesbian persons are indeed among the neighbors we are called by Christ to love. But what that love entails, and the implications for church policy, evoke different responses among us."[18] The draft then indicates three different types of responses toward homosexuality and concludes that the second and the third, both of which affirm same sex genital activity, "are strongly supported by responsible biblical interpretation."[19] These positions may be articulated by innovative interpreters of the Bible but whether they are biblical is another question.

This identical text from Romans 13 is also analyzed in *Veritatis Splendor* and understood in a remarkably unlike way: "When the apostle Paul sums up the fulfillment of the law in the precept of love of neighbor as oneself (cf. Rom. 13:8-10), he is not weakening the commandments but reinforcing them, since he is revealing their requirements and their gravity. Love of God and of one's neighbor cannot be separated from the

17. "The Church and Human Sexuality: A Lutheran Perspective," First Draft of a Social Statement, Division for Church in Society, Department for Studies of the Evangelical Lutheran Church in America [henceforth: ELCA], Chicago, October 1993.

18. ELCA, 15. In the evaluation of this ELCA text that follows it is important to note that the comments are directed to the question of what is normative for Scripture and do not stand in judgment of particular individuals.

19. ELCA, 16.

observance of the commandments of the covenant renewed in the blood of Jesus Christ and in the gift of the Spirit."[20] We will need to return to this glaring example of how the same text can be read so differently in Rome and in Chicago.

In a response that is for the most part supportive of the ELCA study draft on sexuality, a group of faculty from the Luther Northwestern Theological Seminary[21] have argued that "the Bible is not primarily a source of moral teachings. Rather, the Bible is God's means of coming to us."[22] Although one would certainly concur that Scripture cannot be used as a legalistic textbook that describes and prescribes all Christian action, it *is*, however, a foundational source of moral teaching and contains certain parameters of behavior, the performance of which places one outside the community.[23] To argue that the "Bible is God's means of coming to us"[24] engages in a level of abstraction that leads to distortion. The God of Israel and the God of Jesus comes to us incarnate and with a specific intention: for salvation, for the setting right of a broken cosmos, for the healing of sin, for reestablishing relationship with him, and for setting us on a path whereby we, through unmerited grace, can discern and do his will.

A bit further on, LNTS states that "the Bible does indeed inform and guide us in regard to moral issues."[25] But, regrettably, "to inform and guide us" is not meant in any authoritative sense. We are told — incorrectly — that the "church has overridden what has been interpreted as the clear teachings of Scripture in favor of more just practices which better serve the neighbor

---

20. *Veritatis Splendor*, in *Origins* 23/18 (October 14, 1993): 297-336; 320 cited.

21. "A response to *The Church and Human Sexuality: A Lutheran Perspective* by members of the faculty named below at Luther Northwestern Theological Seminary, St. Paul, Minnesota, April 5, 1994." The Faculty Drafting Group includes Robert H. Albers, Terence E. Fretheim, Arland J. Hultgren, Diane L. Jacobson, and Paul R. Sponheim. [Henceforth referred to as LNTS.]

22. LNTS, 1.

23. See, for example, 1 Corinthians 5:1-12.

24. LNTS, 1.

25. LNTS, 2.

and community. The church, for example, remarries divorced persons, ordains women and opposes slavery. . . ."[26] Further, the church is encouraged to incorporate the insights of the natural and social sciences and thus "to exercise our stewardship as persons endowed by reason and powers of observation."[27]

The brief, but representative, citations from both of these documents raise a host of troubling questions:

- What is the teaching authority of Scripture?
- Can the church override the clear teachings of Scripture?
- Can one subscribe to a vague hermeneutic of "love" that no longer specifies the basic conditions for the love of neighbor and is separated from a christological understanding of law?
- Or, is the church permitted to endorse a hermeneutic shaped by "more just practices" and endowments of "reason and powers of observation" divorced from the doctrine of sin?
- Is it the content of Christian Scripture that describes love or does an abstract and inarticulate concept of human love, one that entices us to place the love of neighbor apart from the love of God, shape the church's understanding of Scripture?[28] For some, love seems to be exempt from the corrupting power of sin.
- Does the will of God as revealed in the Christ event correct and inform our reason, powers of observation, and definitions of love *or* do these human perceptions correct and inform our understanding of Scripture?
- Must the church reject not only such a docetic understanding of love but also the correlative Gnostic understanding of Jesus that virtually separates justification from sanctification, grace from a life of discipleship shaped by our freedom from the bondage to sin?

26. LNTS, 3.
27. LNTS, 2.
28. See *Veritatis Splendor*, 302-3.

• It should be noted that the discussion of "law and gospel" is thoroughly confused and confusing in the ELCA Study Draft, the LNTS response, and in many parts of Lutheranism. The time has come to give up these shibboleths and to describe what is intended in a non-ghettoized language that is intelligible to a wider audience and one in dialogue with the biblical studies on the subject.[29]

An Initial Response to the Problem of Alien Hermeneutics

How would an ecclesiological, trinitarian hermeneutic, in which Scripture is recognized as a unified and canonical whole, respond to such interpretations?

With regard to the authority of Scripture, one can assert, together with *Veritatis Splendor*,[30] that "Christ is the teacher, the risen one who has life in himself and who is always present in his church and in the world. It is he who opens up to the faithful the book of the Scriptures and, by fully revealing the Father's will, teaches the truth about moral action." As a result, Scripture is and remains the "living and fruitful source"[31] of the church's ethical and moral teachings. There is in Scripture an intimate and unbreakable bond between justification and sanctification, faith and moral actions that are pleasing to God.[32]

With regard to the apparent separation of faith and the moral life, should one not assert that the way of salvation is, according to Scripture, actualized precisely in the obedience of the moral life? Is this not what Paul means by the "obedience of faith" in Romans (1:5; cf. 6:16; 15:18)? With *Veritatis Splendor* one has to ask whether it is "possible to obey God and thus

---

29. See Childs, *Biblical Theology*, 686-98.
30. *Veritatis Splendor*, 301.
31. *Veritatis Splendor*, 307.
32. This theme is especially stressed in 1 Thessalonians 4:1-8.

love God and neighbor without respecting these command-ments in all circumstances?"[33] In fact, if these commandments are not respected must one not, in fact, speak of the possibility of love as sin? Can an abstract discussion of love override the commandments?

There is a fundamental misconception among many that the divine openness of Christ to all sorts and conditions of persons is equivalent to an "I'm OK, you're OK" mentality. Surely the grace of Christ welcomes all for the purpose of repentance and the renewal of a right relationship with the living God. The message of divine openness, however, also includes a divine invitation to lead a life of discipleship. "Come, follow me" (Matt. 19:21). The indicative contains an imperative! Or, to put it in a Pauline context, justification is both *Gabe und Aufgabe*[34] (gift and responsibility). It is not, there-fore, incidental that much of Scripture, including the New Testament, places great emphasis on paraenesis and urges vig-ilance over the right conduct of the new life in Christ.

Lutherans especially get nervous in such discussions, al-most immediately suggesting that one is engaging in a "works righteousness." So let's listen to Luther: "Good works do not make a good man, but a good man does good works."[35] The life of discipleship cannot be exercised as a result of our own strength but only because a gift has been received. As Paul makes clear in Romans 8:1-4, only in the life of the Spirit is the law, that is, the will of God, fulfilled and the possibility of carrying out God's commandments given. Neither here nor in 1 Corinthians 7, however, do God's commandments become *adiaphora:* "For neither circumcision counts for anything nor uncircumcision, but keeping the commandments of God" (1 Cor. 7:19).

Some responses are in order to the LNTS recommenda-

33. *Veritatis Splendor,* 300.
34. Ernst Käsemann, *New Testament Questions of Today* (Philadelphia: Fortress, 1969), 170.
35. Martin Luther, "A Treatise on Christian Liberty," in *Three Treatises* (Philadelphia: Muhlenberg Press, 1943), 271.

tion that we need a hermeneutic shaped by "more just practices" and endowments of "reason and powers of observation." These proposals urge, in a surprisingly Thomistic way, that ". . . what is needed is the public exercise of human reasoning. . . ."[36] Would not Luther question whether human beings can, without forgiveness and the guidance of the Spirit normed by Scripture, really know what best serves the neighbor, what best enhances life in community, and what is just, and would he not be highly skeptical of placing such a high value on "reason and the powers of observation" insulated from the corrupting power of sin? Would not Luther, based on Augustine and Paul in Romans 3, hold that "reason and the powers of observation" are in bondage to sin? Here, too, one observes the disturbing tendency to separate sanctification from justification, the moral life in Christ from faith, and an ethics, human in origin, placed in opposition to the teaching of the trinitarian church, namely, that the moral life is not established by human beings but by God himself, the Holy Trinity. What is "just" is *authored* by God and not humans, and it is as a result of this divine *author*ship that God's justice and righteousness becomes *author*itative for us.

Since there are echoes of Thomism in the LNTS statement, it would be well to hear a current assessment of human reason from a Christian tradition that places significant value on Saint Thomas and on natural law. "Some people," we are told in *Veritatis Splendor*, by ". . . disregarding the dependence of human reason on divine wisdom and the need, given the present state of fallen nature, for divine revelation as an effective means for knowing moral truths, even those of the natural order, have actually posited a complete sovereignty of reason in the domain of moral norms regarding the right ordering of life in this world."[37]

This same perspective needs to be applied also to the frequent dependence on the behavioral sciences as an authority

36. LNTS, 2.
37. *Veritatis Splendor*, 309.

31

in the moral arena. Must not those who stand in the biblical tradition be at least suspicious that what is declared as "normal" in these human endeavors might also be warped by the power of sin? Can one concur that the hermeneutic which lies at the root of much current thinking in the behavioral sciences — that of an autonomous self, motivated by the need to satisfy personal desire — is incompatible with a life of discipleship? Is experiencing the joy of the gospel dependent on every human need being acted upon? Again, the contemporary Roman Catholic tradition has spoken forthrightly: "The affirmation of moral principles is not within the competence of formal empirical methods. . . . Hence the behavioral sciences, despite the great value of the information which they provide, cannot be considered decisive indications of moral norms. It is the Gospel which reveals the full truth about man and his moral journey, and thus enlightens and admonishes sinners. . . ."[38]

Given, then, this false hermeneutical starting point and the failure to view Scripture as a unified whole and a fruitful source of the church's moral teaching, there is a widespread tendency to play "First-Century Bible Land,"[39] that is, to pick and choose those texts that fit the ideology being developed and to discard those texts that contradict it as obsolete, time-conditioned, or belonging to Jewish or Hellenistic baggage that can be jettisoned. Again, it is necessary to insist that it is not the historical-critical approach that is primarily at fault, but, rather, the hermeneutic that appropriates and interprets its results.[40]

38. *Veritatis Splendor*, 329-30.
39. Krister Stendahl, *The Bible and the Role of Women: A Case Study in Hermeneutics* (Philadelphia: Fortress, 1966), 40.
40. As Joseph Cardinal Ratzinger has pointed out, not even the tools developed and employed by historical critics are without presuppositions. See his analysis, "A Biblical Interpretation in Crisis: On the Question of the Foundations and Approaches of Exegesis Today," in Neuhaus, *Biblical Interpretation in Crisis*, 1-23.

III. The Bible and the Church: Canonical Criticism

What is found in both the LNTS statement and in much of the work of Krister Stendahl,[41] which will be discussed shortly, is an attempt to reduce and synthesize the diversity and irreducible particularity of the canon to a nebulous, docetic encounter with the Word, in which a living conversation with the canon in its entirety is cut short.

Brevard Childs's magisterial *Biblical Theology of the Old and New Testament: Theological Reflection on the Christian Bible*[42] is to be applauded because it challenges the current state of affairs in much that passes for biblical scholarship. Both the fragmentation of the biblical text and its removal from its canonical context are criticized. Yet Childs recognizes that one cannot and should not attempt to turn the clock back as if the historical-critical developments of the late-nineteenth and twentieth centuries had never occurred. Not only is he fully cognizant of the misuses to which these advances have been put, he also applauds some of their significant contributions. Where Childs is to be commended is in his attempt to recognize that both the trajectory leading to the final redaction of texts and their canonical placement are critical if the community of faith is to engage in a conversation with Scripture. To eliminate the first opens the door to a naive fundamentalism or a dogmatic misuse of the coherent gospel articulated in contingent contexts;[43] to ignore the second creates a biblical scholarship fixated at an infantile level based on a fragmented

---

41. See, for example, Krister Stendahl, "Memorandum on Our Bible and Our Sexuality," to be published in a volume sponsored by the Evangelical Lutheran Church in America, 1993.

42. Brevard S. Childs, *Biblical Theology of the Old and New Testaments* (Minneapolis: Fortress, 1993).

43. In using the terms "coherent" and "contingent" I am indebted to the work of J. Christiaan Beker, *Paul the Apostle* (Philadelphia: Fortress, 1980), especially 11-16, although he is not to be held responsible for the particular way in which I use and interpret this terminology.

hermeneutic bound to distort the canonical context of the biblical witness to the reality of the Triune God. When such a fractionalized, alien hermeneutic begins to permeate the various levels of ecclesiastical structure, then Christianity can easily be seduced by well-intentioned ideologies, often camouflaged under an ethic of love, but nonetheless demonic.

To hold in creative tension and to properly interpret the various redactional levels as well as the final canonical form of Scripture requires not only a profound knowledge of the primary text of Scripture but also academic learning and theological insight. Childs displays both, and for that reason alone his most recent volume ought to be read by every serious student of Scripture and theology. Further, Childs is to be lauded for seeing the necessity of both biblical theological reflection based on the discrete witness of both the New *and* the Old Testament, and interaction between such a biblical theology and a dogmatic theology. Childs, in all likelihood, would be the first to admit that he is attempting to get a process underway rather than that he has spoken a final word, if there ever can be such a "final" word short of the kingdom. Thus, the great service of Childs is to point us in the right direction and to begin a long overdue conversation between exegetes and their systematic counterparts in the theological enterprise.

A Canonical Approach to the Study of Sexuality: First Steps

A canonical approach to the study of sexuality, guided by a christological and trinitarian hermeneutic, would need to examine all the relevant witnesses in the Old and the New Testament and then interpret each within the entire theological context of Scripture. The beginning point, therefore, must be to hear the complete witness of Scripture as a whole; to start and end with Romans 1, as is the case in the recent essay by Arland

Hultgren, guarantees distortion.[44] It is Scripture that norms Romans 1:26-28 and not the other way around. Not only must one look at these witnesses both within the specific and the larger theological contexts in which they are found, but there must be attention to (a) the question of God's intention in creation with regard to sexuality, (b) what, biblically, is meant by sin, and (c) the quality of Christian existence "in Christ."

Although it is not our task here to produce a complete perspective on the question of human sexuality in light of biblical theology, at least some directions can be charted. The testimony of Jesus in Mark 10:2-12 is an appropriate starting point. Since these words contain a clear reference back to the intention of God in creation and explicitly cite Genesis 1 and 2, it is necessary to examine these texts in Genesis dealing with God's creation of man and woman as sexual beings. Then all other appropriate texts need to be examined, including Genesis 19:1-29; Leviticus 18:22; 20:13; Matthew 19:3-12; 1 Corinthians 6:9-11; 1 Timothy 1:10; Romans 1:18-32; Ephesians 5:21-33.

In examining these and other texts we are not only attempting to do so in the context of Scripture as a unified and canonical whole, but also recognizing them as contingent[45] texts spoken in specific historical moments and situations. In order to understand their intention one must be alert to the countercultural thrust that is inherent in them. All of these investigations will be considerably aided, then, by a combined canonical/historical-critical approach. In listening to the whole of Scripture all relevant texts must be examined and listened to with care; one must be very careful about prejudgments that wish to jettison certain texts because of their cultic context (Leviticus), or because they are part of Paul's Jewish-Hellenistic past (for example, Romans 1) or because they contain a so-called view of "subordination" that is no longer fashionable today (for example, Ephesians 5).

---

44. Hultgren, "Being Faithful."

45. By the term "contingent" is meant the specific actualization of the salvific will of God; it does not refer to something as irrelevant or as "discardable."

Often the ideological imperialisms of the day short-circuit the first step of any responsible biblical interpretation, namely, inquiring into the author's primary intention in writing what he does at a given historical moment.

No text can be approached without presuppositions,[46] and we are not unaware that we ourselves live in a culture that trivializes sex at all levels. It is hardly coincidental that "permissive abortion, widespread adultery, easy divorce, radical feminism, and the gay and lesbian movement . . . [have] appeared at the same historical moment."[47] What follow, then, in the light of this situation, are some questions and theses that might emerge as one attempts to be in dialogue with these biblical texts, realizing that the text of Scripture might lead to a rejection, modification, or confirmation of the appropriateness of one's presuppositions.

Mark 10:2-12. After having been in careful conversation with the text, together with its synoptic parallels in Matthew and Luke, and having noted their obvious dependence on Genesis, one must ask whether the thesis of Wolfhart Pannenberg can be affirmed: "Jesus' words in Mark 10:2-9 allow the following conclusion: that the goal of the Creator's intention for humanity is the undeviating fellowship of husband and wife. The indissoluble fellowship of marriage is the reason for the creation of humans as sexual beings."[48]

Genesis 1:27-28. Can one affirm with Rodney Hutton that according to Genesis 1 sexual differentiation "was viewed as a divine gift, a mark of blessing, and a responsibility faithfully to be lived out as God's co-creators"?[49] If God's gift of sexuality

---

46. See the insightful article by Rudolf Bultmann, "Is Exegesis Without Presuppositions Possible?" in *Existence and Faith: Shorter Writings of Rudolf Bultmann,* ed. Schubert M. Ogden, 289-96.

47. "The Homosexual Movement: A Response by the Ramsey Colloquium," in *First Things* 41 (March 1994): 17.

48. Wolfhart Pannenberg, " 'Einem männlichen Wesen darfst du nicht beiwohnen,' Maßstäbe zur kirchlichen Urteilsbildung über Homosexualität," *Zeitwende* 65/1 (January 1994): 1 [translation mine].

49. Rodney Hutton, "Old Testament Perspectives on Human Sexuality" [unpublished typescript], 8.

is also a call to be responsible to him as co-creators, it would suggest that this particular ethical issue has to be high on the church's list of moral concerns, for what is being called for is fidelity to the work of God himself both in community and creation.

Genesis 2:18-25. One will wish to inquire from this text whether the primary significance of this relationship between male and female resides not in the procreative potential of this relationship "but rather in its sexual nature at a deeper level. The two are opposites who confront one another and who bring each other into completion."[50] Is it not the perspective of the Old Testament that such a complementary relationship is only capable of expression heterosexually and that therefore homosexual relationships are viewed as contrary to God's purpose for the human situation? Hutton would even go further and urge that the "aversion to homosexual practice in the Old Testament is certainly anchored in some sense of the ordered nature of creation — that Adam was given this opposite who is yet of his very bone and flesh. She is woman because she was taken from man."[51] Would a careful probing and reflection on this text in its canonical entirety shed insight into such troublesome texts as 1 Corinthians 11 dealing with the ordering of creation and possibly suggest that the core issue for Paul cannot be described as "hierarchical" but "relational"?[52]

Can Genesis 1 and 2 be read apart from Genesis 3 and the reality of sin? Sexuality in both Testaments is repeatedly described as a gift that is not simply "dysfunctional" but something that has been distorted and perverted by the power of sin. In Scripture sexuality is a sign of brokenness because of sin. According to the witness of Scripture, sin is not simply the

---

50. Hutton, "Old Testament Perspectives," 13-14.

51. Hutton, "Old Testament Perspectives," 13.

52. *kephalē* is not concerned with "head" as authority, but as the source of life. Although man is the source of woman's life, she is man's glory without whom he would not be complete — remarkably parallel to Genesis 2:18-25. See further Gordon D. Fee, *The First Epistle to the Corinthians* (Grand Rapids: Eerdmans, 1987), 498-512.

result of personal choice, in which the autonomous self is the sole arbiter of moral authority; rather, sin is an evil force reflecting "the power of chaos lying caged beneath God's created world."[53] Only when the chaotic and transpersonal nature of sin is taken seriously, can one begin to understand how the partnership between male and female, created out of opposition for the purpose of complementarity, can be disfigured into alienation and oppression. To argue that something is not sinful because it has not been chosen is a radical mutilation of the biblical affirmation and, to use the language of the Pastoral Epistles (Tit. 2:1), sets individual freedom in opposition to sound doctrine.

Romans 1:26-28. In the context of this discussion it is relevant to make reference to Romans 1:26-28 since it is frequently asserted that Paul is not here referring to persons with a homosexual orientation but those homosexual acts committed by *heterosexual* persons who "exchanged" natural intercourse for unnatural. This is a misreading of the text; Paul has no interest whatsoever in individual decisions or matters of sexual orientation. The Apostle intends only to describe the condition of sinful Gentiles who have exchanged the truth about God for a lie (1:25). Ancients did not think that there was a class of people with sexual "preferences" for the same sex. This notion that there is a "class" of people characterized by their sexual preference is a most recent notion and one that has no basis in the Western tradition. Thus, to try to use it as an interpretative category promotes misunderstanding and to apply it to Paul is a classic example of "eisegesis." Those interpreters who impose this argument on the text attempt thereby to deploy the text for their reconstruction of what Paul *really* meant and, in turn, dismiss the interpretation that the church fathers and the vast majority of modern commentators give to it. In addition it is necessary to contend that for Paul homosexual practice is not merely a matter of specific, private sexual acts; these acts have moral and communal impact. By undermining the

53. Hutton, "Old Testament Perspectives," 22.

union of male and female, which is at the heart of the Creator's intention, homosexual practices alienate human beings from one another and from God. "Paul," according to E. P. Sanders, "condemns both male and female homosexuality in blanket terms and without making any distinctions."[54] This is exactly the point that Paul is making in Romans 1 and in 1 Corinthians 6:9-11.[55]

Leviticus 18:6-23 and 20:13; Genesis 19:1-11. The urgent questions that must be raised with regard to these texts are (a) whether Leviticus 18 and 20 can be dismissed because they are merely "cultic" and (b) whether Genesis 19 is really dealing with inhospitality rather than sexually offensive behavior. Using both a historical-critical and a canonical approach, it must be asked, on the one hand, on what basis one is able to dismiss the warrants against male homosexuality but not those dealing with incest and bestiality, and, on the other hand, whether the remainder of the canon actually understands Genesis 19:1-11 merely as inhospitality. Both the use of the verb *yada* in Genesis[56] as "having sexual intercourse" and the reference in Ezekiel 16:47-52 to the Sodom tradition as the doing of "abominable things" make clear that sexual offenses, and specifically, homosexual activity, are the focus.[57] An examination of the entire biblical witness, including not only Ezekiel 16:47-52 but also Jeremiah 23:14; Isaiah 1:9; 13:19; Amos 4:11;

54. E. P. Sanders, *Paul* (Oxford: Oxford University Press, 1991), 112-13.
55. With regard to the use of the terms *malakoi* and *arsenokoitai*, Sanders, *Paul,* 112-13, comments: "Paul names both the effeminate partner, the *malakos,* 'soft' one, and the active one, the *arsenokoites.* Some scholars propose that the words are uncertain as to meaning and thus that perhaps Paul did not really condemn homosexuality. The words, however, are quite clear. 'Soft' was a common term for the passive partner, and nothing could be more explicit than 'one who buggers males'. We noted the word in the Sibylline Oracles 2:73, and both that passage and Paul's reflect the terminology of Leviticus 18:22 and 20:13: *meta arsenos koiten,* 'he who has coitus with a male.'"
56. Genesis 4:1, 17, 25; 24:16; 38:26.
57. Hutton, "Old Testament Perspectives," 18: *to eba* in Ezekiel 16:50a is the same term used for homosexual activity in Leviticus 18:22 and 20:13.

Zephaniah 2:9; Jude 7; 2 Peter 2:4-8; Matthew 11:23-24, makes it difficult to sustain the argument that the reference to Sodom and Gomorrah is ever primarily cited as an example of "inhospitality." Rather, the themes of "total destruction" and "sexual offense" are the ones in the foreground.

A canonical study of sexuality will, after exploring all of these texts in detail and in conversation with one another, have to ask whether, in fact, the Old Testament's negative understanding of "homoerotic behavior is consistent and is coherent with its view of the nature of God's intent for sexual expression within the context of patterns of justice and righteousness which permeate creation."[58] Also to be explored is the Pauline theme of justification as God's sovereign reclamation and restoration of his broken creation and whether the Apostle is not precisely setting the revelation of God's righteousness in Jesus Christ (Rom. 3:21-31) over against the sinfulness described in Romans 1:18-32.

Our own preliminary reading of this biblical material tends in these directions:

1. That marriage is linked with the procreative power of and responsibility to the Creator God; that marriage represents the complementariness of male and female; that marriage is the only arena for the expression of sexual desire, a desire that is powerful and often unpredictable. Consistent with this reading of Scripture, the Ramsey colloquium urges that marriage "is a place where, in a singular manner, our waywardness begins to be healed and our fear of commitment overcome, where we may learn to place another person's needs rather than our own desires at the center of life."[59]

2. That there is not one biblical text that contradicts Paul's negative evaluation of homosexuality; that homosexuality is repeatedly declared to be a path that deviates from God's creational intentionality; and, finally, that today's cultural sit-

58. Hutton, "Old Testament Perspectives," 21.
59. "The Homosexual Movement: A Response by the Ramsey Colloquium," 17.

uation is not new: Paul unwaveringly speaks against a culture with a radically divergent sexual ethic.

IV. Concluding Observations

To bring some of the observations just made into sharper focus and to test their accuracy and persuasiveness, one ought to compare them with the work of Krister Stendahl, his book and article on hermeneutics, his fall 1993 lecture to clergy on the West Coast as well as his current "Memorandum on Our Bible and Our Sexuality" written for a volume being published by the ELCA.[60]

1. Basic to his various writings is the distinction between "what it meant," "what it means," and "what it might come to mean."[61] This seems quite automatically to set up a fracture between the authority of Scripture as understood by the church fathers and the contemporary church. Is there not here a fundamental flaw in perception? Does not the essential message of the gospel remain unchanged? Is not the difference that Stendahl is trying to convey more accurately expressed through use of the categories "coherent" and "contingent"? Stendahl's proper concern is not to "freeze" the contingent into the absolute. While recognizing the significance of this point, it must, however, be emphasized that there are fundamental witnesses to truth in Scripture that are not up for grabs as a result of either the indeterminate argument of contingency or as a consequence of the ideological winds that sweep across every generation. What is more accurate than the "what it meant"/"what it means" dichotomy is the recognition that there is a difference between "the truths of faith and the man-

---

60. See notes 40 and 41 above.

61. Krister Stendahl, "Biblical Theology, Contemporary," in the *Interpreter's Dictionary of the Bible* (Nashville: Abingdon, 1962), I:418-32 and now reprinted with new introductory remarks in *Meanings: The Bible as Document and as Guide* (Philadelphia: Fortress, 1984), 11-44; see also 1-7.

ner in which they are expressed. . . ."[62] Contingent articulation, however, does not negate the truth of faith expressed.

2. Stendahl sets up an unwarranted disjunction between the Old and the New Testament. Although acknowledging that procreation is an important dimension of sexuality in the Old Testament, the "theme of procreation is not part of Paul's reasoning about sexuality, nor is it anywhere in the New Testament."[63] Does Stendahl assume that Jesus and Paul began with a *tabula rasa* and that the community of Jesus was a new religion begun *de novo?* It is indeed puzzling that the one who has argued so vigorously against such a view and who has repeatedly urged that Paul was called to a new task and not converted to a new religion, can so hastily drop Paul's Jewishness when it does not fit the needs of his liberationist hermeneutic.

3. Since for Stendahl, procreation is "not a primary factor," current moral arguments with regard to sexuality "must find new grounding in those principles of fidelity and mutuality."[64] Not only is this fundamental thesis about procreation incorrect since all generations participate with God in the responsibility of "co-creation," but the terms "fidelity and mutuality" are removed from their biblical context of creation. In addition, "mutuality" quickly degenerates into a polemic against the so-called "hierarchy of male and female"[65] in the New Testament. One reason, it is alleged, why many are uneasy about lesbians is that they threaten such a hierarchical structure. What texts does Stendahl have in mind here? 1 Corinthians 11?[66] It is difficult to imagine how this kind of analysis can stand up to exegetical scrutiny; it appears to be a form of historical imagination that is more Gnostic than biblical.

62. *Veritatis Splendor,* 307.
63. Stendahl, "Memorandum," 4.
64. Stendahl, "Memorandum," 5.
65. Stendahl, "Memorandum," 6.
66. See the comments made with regard to this text on page 16 above.

4. Stendahl's ideological hermeneutic skillfully plays the game of "First-Century Bible Land" when it suits his purposes even though he remonstrates against this sport![67] He reminds us that in 1 Corinthians 7:10 and 12, Paul is giving advice to a specific situation in Corinth and clearly states, "I say, not the Lord. . . ." These statements become, for Stendahl, Paul's "personal opinions" and his "tentative advice"[68] and are then applied to Romans 1:26-28 and 1 Corinthians 6:9-11. These clever exegetical maneuvers conflate contingency with coherence and essentially erode Scripture as a normative source for theology and ethics. What is to stop us from applying these "personal opinions" and "tentative advice" to the theme of the resurrection and simply conflate the contingency of apocalyptic language with the divine mystery of resurrection and discard them both as outdated cultural expressions? Any canonical exegesis will want to present all of the relevant texts within the total framework of the testimony of Scripture; only within this broader field of meaning can one discuss matters of contingency and coherence. Stendahl's grave hesitancy to follow such a hermeneutic is also evident when he uses Matthew 23:4 to warn the ELCA against "binding heavy burdens" with regard to sexuality, a text that has absolutely nothing to do with marriage, divorce, or celibacy. The danger of picking and choosing texts to fit into various liberationist hermeneutics is evident in much of the debris that passes for biblical exegesis today.

These concluding observations, made by one in the biblical field, do have theological consequences for pastors and systematicians, consequences that need to be carefully evaluated. The challenges issued might be summarized in the following way:

1. If one more correctly talks about "coherence/contingency" rather than "what it meant/what it means," then it would follow that there are some moral commandments that will always prohibit certain types of behavior in their attempt to describe a life "worthy of the gospel of Christ" (Phil. 1:27).

---

67. See note 52 above.
68. Stendahl, "Memorandum," 2.

43

2. If the interpretative key for a christologically based trinitarian ecclesiological hermeneutic is always the crucified and risen Christ, then any claims for liberation and freedom must be tested against the freedom to which Christ calls us in discipleship. For the church to defend unchanging moral norms is not an expression of oppression but an exercise in defending the true freedom of the Christian, a freedom gained only by the death of the crucified one whose service is perfect freedom. Thus, ambiguous calls to liberation can never stand in opposition to revelational truth. It is not some modern notion of freedom that becomes the source of our ethical life, but the will of God as testified to in Scripture and interpreted by the trinitarian church.

3. Since the church and its development of the canon is not a later addendum to the Christ event but an intrinsic part of it, any modern theological treatment of sexuality will need to review the struggle of the church over many centuries with this issue, a struggle set forth powerfully by Peter Brown in his extraordinary volume *Body and Society*.[69] Were early Christians, one must ask, simply perverse in their struggle with sexuality or did they correctly recognize in it a power that, if not exercised with great care, could have demonic consequences? Did they perhaps have an insight that we postmoderns might benefit from today, namely, that sexual activity must not become the dominating center of human existence?

Finally, my own biblical/theological observations on the theme of sexuality cohere remarkably with the theological/biblical reflections of Wolfhart Pannenberg, and I submit them to you for your consideration and reflection: "Whoever pressures the church to alter the normativeness of its teaching with regard to homosexuality must be aware that that person promotes schism in the church. For a church that would permit itself to be pressured to no longer understand homosexual activity as a deviation from the biblical norm and to recognize

69. Peter Brown, *The Body and Society: Men, Women, and Sexual Renunciation in Early Christianity* (New York: Columbia University Press, 1988).

homosexual partnerships alongside of marriage, such a church would no longer be based on the foundation of Scripture, but, rather, in opposition to its unanimous witness. A church that moves in such a direction would therefore have ceased being an evangelical church following in the steps of the Lutheran Reformation."[70] It is hoped that a declaration as forthright as this will provoke a much needed and long overdue dialogue concerning the essential characteristics of a hermeneutic necessary to reclaim the Bible for the church.

70. Pannenberg, "Maßstäbe zur kirchlichen Urteilsbildung über Homosexualität," 4 [translation mine].

The Loss of Biblical Authority and Its Recovery

ROY A. HARRISVILLE

There is no use to cavil at the statement that the Bible has been lost to the church; no use to say that our perspective is too limited to allow its universal application to the one holy, catholic and apostolic church; that the loss of the Bible may hold true only of a certain portion of it, not even of all of that, but only the slice of it of which you or I have any experience. There's good reason for generalizing on a particular here, since, in the New Testament at least, the entire body of Christ, and nothing left over, may be situated at Corinth or Galatia or Rome or Newark or Northfield. We have precedent for stating here, in this place, that the Bible has been lost to the church. As for the word "church," it may refer to any and all willy-nilly, whether or not they confess it or simply derive their income from researching it. An acquaintance once said to me, "I don't give a damn what the church thinks; John D. Rockefeller pays my salary." But he would have had to earn his keep by other means — at least, until he moved to the history department of his university — had not John D. Rockefeller been a Baptist.

ROY A. HARRISVILLE

How Has the Bible Been Lost?

One answer to this question is that the loss has been in its authority, an authority often construed in terms of something external, exerting pressure from the outside, something akin to a law. Time was, it is said, when all that was needed to inhibit or prescribe was to point to what the Bible said. When Abraham Lincoln first ran for office, members of the opposition party, anxious to ruin his chances for election, decided upon the charge that he was a freethinker. Lincoln dismissed the charge in a handout attesting to his fidelity to the biblical witness. He lost the election, but for other reasons. In one way or another, pointing to the Bible settled matters. In that sense, conceived as external authority, the Bible has in fact been lost to the church. But then, as I see it, the authority of the Bible has never been merely external. Even those groups that have construed the Bible after the analogy of the deity — inerrant, free of contradiction — even they have hastened to add another, deeper reason for the Bible's authority. And on this point, those of us who have been poles apart on other matters have agreed, and still agree.

Ultimately, the authority of the Bible stems from its self-authentication in the heart and mind of believers. At bottom, the Scriptures of Old and New Testaments derive their authority as sole and final rule for faith and life from their power to evoke assent and trust, to wring a "yes! yes!" from deep inside their readers and hearers; such power as to cut them adrift from whatever allegiances they once may have owed; to render them without ideology, without a metaphysic or political programme, to suspend them between heaven and hell without a single "ism" to their name, to turn them into what any secularist with half a brain would call atheists, risking everything on words whose truths resist establishing by human act or logic. And the loss of *this* authority is far worse, more tragic than simply the loss of any external authority. We had best be clear about it: The Bible is lost to the church in terms of its power to evoke the resolve to live or die by it.

48

How did it happen, *this* loss? In the words of an old Trojan in Vergil's *Aeneid:*

> We made a breach in the walls, and laid open the bulwarks of the city. . . . The fatal machine passed over our walls, pregnant with arms; boys and unmarried virgins accompanied it with sacred hymns. . . . It advanced, and with menacing aspect slid into the heart of the city. . . . Four times it stopped in the very threshold of the gate, and four times the arms resounded in its womb: yet we, heedless, and blind with frantic zeal, urged on, and planted the baneful monster in the sacred citadel. . . . [And] The towering horse, planted in the midst of our streets, poured forth armed troops. . . .

The "fatal machine" was a method of research spawned from an age that put off fear of God but maintained a respectful attitude toward the deity; renounced the authority of church and Bible but exhibited a faith in the authority of nature and reason; dismantled heaven but retained faith in the immortality of the soul; denied that miracles ever happened but believed in the perfectibility of the human race. These opposites, cited in Carl Becker's 1930 lectures to the Yale Law School, will do for a description of the Enlightenment, the age that has furnished most of the grist for whatever mills have been grinding in this country over the last two hundred years.

Was the act malicious? It was no more malicious than the Trojans' reception of that "towering horse." Part of the story of biblical criticism in this country yet to be told, or told with accuracy, is that it was the "good guys" who first introduced us to that business of advancing beyond the mere restoration of the biblical text to questions concerning its orality, integrity, religious-historical context, and authenticity. On a bright, sunny day in 1812, when Napoleon was getting the comeuppance celebrated in almost every college or university or municipal concert hall in the Western world for the last hundred years, and with varying degrees of success, a true-blue trinitarian from Andover, Moses Stuart, fell to reading

Johann Gottfried Eichhorn's *Introduction to the Old Testament*. From then on he was candidate for the "higher criticism," and it was soon whispered that this preserver of the doctrines of the Trinity and the person of Christ for evangelical faith, whose *Letters to the Rev. William Ellery Channing* were hailed as orthodoxy's frontline defense against the unitarian rabble, had not only gone over to the Germans but was taking his students with him, infecting them with deistical rationalism; and that it was all his colleagues could do to keep the school from tumbling into unitarianism.

History does not mention Charles Augustus Briggs of New York, another believer, vilified for his research and made the occasion for splitting the presbytery of his state, or William Smith of Aberdeen, who believed with all his heart that the Triune God is present in the history to which Christian tradition binds us no less than to any critical historical description, and who was damned for a heretic and removed from his chair. Good guys, believers, *not* sniggering philosophers, had "planted the baneful monster in the sacred citadel." The story of the entry of historical criticism into this country is the story of Joseph upside down: "You meant it unto me for good, but God meant it unto me for evil."

Couldn't the Stuarts and the Briggses have guessed at the consequences likely to be drawn from their allegiance to critical method? Stuart would have choked at the suggestion of a company of "Fellows," exceeding the mythical seventy of Septuagint lore by three, and advertising itself as representing a "wide array of Western religious traditions and academic institutions"; at the idea that "the sage from Nazareth" had been smothered by the mythical Christ of the creeds; or at such noxious words as the boast at a conference anachronistically titled "Reimaginings" that nothing was accomplished in the name of the Trinity, to the accompaniment of laughter and cheers.

How Can the Bible Be Reclaimed?

Shall we abandon the method?

Eight years ago, the German scholar Eta Linnemann published a volume in which she repudiated everything she had written to that date — her books on the parables and passion narrative, her contributions to magazines, to books of essays, and to *Festschriften*. She had come to believe that all biblical research occurred within a context that determined its direction beforehand, that a series of basic presuppositions formed a filter through which all work had to pass, and that whatever freedom existed lay only within that restricted space. She insisted that even when such presuppositions fell away, the stability of the conception was preserved; it still lived, conserved, encapsulated, at the edge of consciousness. Describing the more than five centuries of Western history together with its worldwide influence as the "pathway of sin," and decrying Augustine's description of Christian use of pagan science as analogous to Israelite plundering of Egyptian goods, she warned of the demonic powers lying in wait for all who struck out on that pathway. It was a way that relegated faith to the private sphere and left no room for the living God and his Son in academic thought. She concluded:

> I am so thankful that the blood of Jesus has washed away my sins! Of course, I was not any better, but worse. . . . But just as I resist divorce in the name of Jesus, I also resist historical-critical theology and call to my Savior in my distress.

And since, she added, the claim to being scientific was an offense against the first commandment, students of theology had best abandon the existing university institutions. What Eta Linnemann went on to substitute for historical-critical method coheres with her repudiation of it.[1]

---

1. Eta Linnemann, *Wissenschaft oder Meinung?* (Neuhausen-Stuttgart: Hänssler, 1986), 26, 60, 75, 88-89, 97, 110-16.

Shall we repair the method?

1. Others embrace measures less extreme than Linnemann's. One Rhenish scholar prefers repair to rejection. He writes that an idea of science engineered by a worldview that leaves no room for God is unscientific, since it excludes solidarity with "all thinking persons." The method, therefore, should consist of establishing findings that all thinking persons can adopt once they have critically tested them. The sentiment is a healthy one. As one of our own wrote more than a century ago in *The Popular Science Monthly:* "Since logic is rooted in the social principle, to be logical men should not be selfish." But what remains of the method following this scholar's repair is strikingly similar to Linnemann's substitution.

2. Peter Stuhlmacher of Tübingen offers a more sophisticated alternative. He insists on the indispensability of historical-critical method, and roundly reproves its detractors. He writes that a rejection of the method or its tailoring to what once was called the "lower criticism" spells surrender of the church's claim to any scientific basis for its exegesis; it spells the substitution of a spiritual, self-evident biblical exposition within the circle of the reborn, a practice come to grief a hundred times in the church's history from gnosticism to every shade of fanaticism. Asserting the indispensability of the method as well as its limits, he appeals for an expansion of the method in an "effective-historical consciousness" — the term belongs to Hans-Georg Gadamer. So, to the principles of criticism, analogy, and correlation once enunciated by Ernst Troeltsch of Berlin he adds a fourth, called the "principle of hearing," that is, a view of history and reality open to transcendence and climaxing in faith in the Bible's inspiration. Here is a principle, he believes, that will yield a consciousness of effects without robbing the historian of the necessity for critically examining his texts.

    Criticisms of Peter Stuhlmacher have been many and severe. One contemporary speaks of his hermeneutics as undermining methodical work and being subjectively arbitrary, as overvaluing tradition and undervaluing the positive force of rational criticism, as harmonizing and obscuring reflection on value, and as spelling romantic recourse to the past.[2] His old doctor-father exclaims that of all the possibilities open to him, Stuhlmacher had to take on ballast from his pietistic past (Käsemann). I am less interested in what separates Stuhlmacher from his critics than in what unites them — an allegiance, however qualified, to a tradition of thought refracted in those principles set down by the great systematician of the History of Religions school, Ernst Troeltsch. As I understand the dogma, every event under the sun in some fashion coheres with every other, for which reason it may be viewed in analogy with every other, and depending upon the degree of manifest coherence, may be held to or disposed of in criticism. Thus, no two events of roughly the same character and occurring in roughly the same part of the world and at roughly the same period in history can have occurred without dependence upon each other. For example, if the proverb in Mark 2:17, "Those who are well have no need of a physician, but those who are sick," should be attested in secular sources, the obvious conclusion is that "words borrowed from the fund of common lore . . . are . . . put on the lips of Jesus."[3] If Buddha said it backwards and Jesus said it forwards, but Buddha said it first, Jesus must have taken it from Buddha and merely stood it on its head. But the world I look out on is far too random a place to allow for such coherence. I would rather not include the monism of an Ernst Troeltsch in any attempt at repair.

2. Manfred Oeming, *Gesamt biblische Theologien der Gegenwart*, Zweite, verbesserte Auflage (Stuttgart: W. Kohlhammer, 1987), 119-34.

3. Robert W. Funk, Roy W. Hoover, and the Jesus Seminar, *The Five Gospels: The Search for the Authentic Words of Jesus* (New York: Macmillan, 1993), 22.

What Needs to Be Done?

What needs to occur in order to reclaim what has been lost to us? First, I believe we need to distinguish. Everything, said Luther, and said it more than once, everything depends on distinguishing. We need to distinguish method from the climate of opinion that has given birth to it or still drives it. I do not share the pessimism that insists that the answers that New Testament criticism gives to historical questions necessarily derive from bias; that if a critic approaches a text with the belief that it is the creation of the early Christian community, it will be so interpreted, or, if it is assumed that the words of the Lord have been faithfully remembered and passed on, criteria will be found to support that contention. It is true — the most dissident voices, beginning with that of Albert Schweitzer, have insisted that the only Jesus the critic can find is the Jesus he already knows. But the fact that biblical scholars have seldom demonstrated the desire or the talent for it does not mean it is impossible to distinguish historical method from whatever philosophical assumptions may be fused with it. And, will Eta Linnemann's identification of the historical-critical method with infidelity to Jesus Christ and her substitution of a discernment of God's saving plan and a gathering of the treasures of the biblical record through humble prayer be of any help at all to those for whom, say, the miracles of the New Testament are at first sight alien and full of riddles? I do not believe the problem lies so much in the sources or the method of their reading as in what one scholar has called "cumbersome philosophical luggage — a medley of inadequate and misleading views of knowledge and objectivity."

Second, presuppositions that have been regnant among us need abandoning — that baggage with which our methods have so long been identified and for that reason have frightened off many a good head. To illustrate, let me refer to a work so far only alluded to: *The Five Gospels: The Search for the Authentic Words of Jesus,* by Robert Funk, Roy Hoover, and the Jesus Seminar. The volume deserves reference because of the number of scholars involved in its preparation, and because of their claim to represent scholarship "that has come to prevail in all the great universities of the world."[4]

1. One assumption that needs rejecting is that the academic must know what cannot be known. According to members of the Seminar, the gnostic Gospel of Thomas and the second synoptic source "Q" provide a "control group" for analyzing the sayings of Jesus in the other, canonical Gospels.[5] But the absence of any argument or evidence for the early dating of Thomas so as to render it a legitimate control hides what one writer has dubbed a "recoil from cognitive dissonance," in other words, fear of acknowledging ignorance. The date of composition of the gnostic Gospel of Thomas is moot, as are the provenance and contents of that elusive source "Q." The note that the sexton found in the pulpit next to the preacher's Bible has often enough characterized our enterprise: "Argument weak, yell like hell."

2. A second assumption that needs ditching is that helpful devices are meant to be hard-and-fast rules. According to members of the Seminar, the contrast between "Christian language or viewpoint and the language or viewpoint of Jesus is a very important clue to the real voice of Jesus."[6] As I remember, the scholar who first, or at least most clearly, urged the criterion of dissimilarity, made it quite clear that it exercised a heuristic function, not intended to be employed as a rule, since it was obvious that things Christians said could have been said by Jesus (!). But use of the criterion of dissimilarity as a hard-and-fast rule is calculated to remove Jesus not only from "the Christian facade of the Christ."[7] It is also designed to remove him from Judaism, since not a single eschatological or apocalyptic utterance is left him. This moved a recent reviewer to muse that "one would have thought that the tragic events of our century might have warned us to be wary of biblical

4. *The Five Gospels*, 35.
5. *The Five Gospels*, 15, 26.
6. *The Five Gospels*, 24.
7. *The Five Gospels*, 2, cf. 7.

scholars who deny the Jewishness of Jesus."[8] Construing what *might* be as what *must* be is a bias, a prejudice needing disposal.

Another aspect attaches to this criterion of dissimilarity, so rigidly used. By deriving the genuineness of a word of Jesus from its uniqueness, genuineness is identified with novelty, an identification originating from two of the unlikeliest sources: students of comparative religions and fundamentalists. Anxious over the loss of Jesus as "firstest with the mostest," since everything he said or did had already been proved to have been said or done by others, the former located Jesus' uniqueness in his attitude toward God, his "religion," while the latter ruled out all similarity with other religious figures as fraud. But study of the New Testament concept of "newness" forces one to abandon the notion of novelty as a fundamental theological category or criterion for historical judgment. The "new" is new not only from the perspective of time, but also from the perspective of quality. The Jesus Seminar, characteristically, assigns the logion in Matthew 13:52 to the later community: "Every scribe who has been trained for the kingdom of heaven is like a householder who brings out of his treasure what is new and what is old."

3. Still another presupposition that needs abandoning is that knowing is like seeing. Funk et al. write that "the Christ of creed and dogma . . . can no longer command the assent of those who have seen the heavens through Galileo's telescope" (that piece of lyrical prose is oddly reminiscent of Bultmann's 1941 essay on the New Testament and mythology); they write that historical reason means "distinguishing the factual from the fictional"; that "to be a *critical* scholar means to make empirical, factual evidence — evidence open to confirmation by independent, neutral observers — the controlling factor in historical judgments."[9] The assumption that neutral observation of data allegedly perceptible to the senses determines

8. In Richard Hays, "The Corrected Jesus," *First Things* 37 (November 1993): 47.

9. *The Five Gospels*, 2, 34.

what is historical and what is not hides a staggering naïveté. It is certainly one thing to distinguish our methods from whatever ideas or notions might drive them on, and quite another to separate them altogether. It is certainly one thing to warn against ancient prejudices that cripple our work and quite another to imagine that we can be absolutely free of all preconceptions, can ever be "neutral." The idea of "self-contained facts floating in non-entity," confirmable through neutral observation, is a colossal presupposition, and in the last 150 years it has been dealt so many blows and from so many quarters — our libraries are bursting with tales of its bludgeoning — that one would have thought it had little strength left to bleat. Years ago, William James wrote:

> One's conviction that the evidence one goes by is of the real objective brand, is only one more subjective opinion added to the lot. For what a contradictory array of opinions have objective evidence and absolute certitude been claimed! . . . There is indeed nothing which some one has not thought absolutely true, while his neighbor deemed it absolutely false; and not an absolutist among them seems ever to have considered that the trouble may all the time be essential, and that the intellect, even with truth directly in its grasp, may have no infallible signal for knowing whether it be truth or no.[10]

The Jesus Seminar has been rattling around in the emptiness of a bankrupt philosophical tradition.

4. A too sanguine trust in the capacity of our tools of reconstruction needs jettisoning. It has long been a source of wonder to literary historians that form critics believe they can move backwards from the written records of the Gospels through various stages of alleged developments so as to arrive at earlier phases of the traditions about Jesus, analyze them,

---

10. William James, *Essays on Faith and Morals* (New York: Longmans, Green, 1947), 47.

and pronounce judgments on their genuineness.[11] With all their delight in its discovery, at least two pioneers in form-critical method never ventured to arrive at such judgments. A hammer is an eminently useful tool, but other tools are also needed for building a house. Yet, when the Jesus Seminar states that it has gathered what is known about oral tradition so as to arrive at rules for determining what Jesus actually said, and in that includes the idea that oral memory begins with single aphorisms or parables, it reflects nineteenth-century ideology regarding the development of culture. In this view, culture develops from the simple form to the complex, from anthropoidal grunts to poetry and prose, from mythology to metaphysics, and from orality to the written word. The transmission of tradition in oral form belongs in the category of the simple, not the complex, because of the human memory on which it depends; assigning to orality what is complex means taxing the memory beyond its capacity to function. Now that idea may be true — although originating from those who imagined themselves to be the apogee of the biological evolution of the race — or it may be false. But the degree of doubt attaching to it requires circumspect use of whatever methods result from it.

Third, we need to wave goodbye to the current denial of extratextual reference. Time was when exegesis was defined as reiterating in my own speech what the author intended to say to his readers or hearers; when only what was historically conditioned was to be replaced by my own language or conceptuality.[12] The Reformer wrote: "First of all, we must learn the language, and know what Paul means by these words: law, sin, grace, faith, righteousness, flesh, spirit and the like; otherwise there is no use to reading." But in these last days, the

11. Cf. Roland Mushat Frye, "Literary Criticism and Gospel Criticism," *Theology Today* 36 (July 1979): 207-219.

12. Willi Marxsen, "Der Beitrag der wissenschaftlichen Exegese des Neuen Testaments für die Verkündigung," *Exegese und Verkündigung;* Zwei Vorträge (München: O. Kaiser, 1957), 50.

mind of the author is dismissed as an "intentional fallacy," irrelevant to interpretation. I have no idea if those who are so eager to give authorial intention a bad name are aware of the genesis of their position or its consequences. It arises from a love affair with science and a disgust for all the ways we have thought in till now. It advertises a world beneath the world we see, a "more real" world of genes and DNA that reduces the world we see to an illusion. It is the "real world" deep beneath the world of common sense. In it there are no referents beyond our words, nothing beyond them to which they point, hence no possibility of matching words to things. The words in a sentence relate only to other words in a sentence, and whatever those words intend is exhausted in that relation; whatever they mean, they mean only in that relation. And since that is so, there is no need for someone who knows what he means, or thinks he knows what he means; there is no need for an "I," for a self, but as one critic writes, there is just "a cloud of momentary energies always in process of fission."[13] In this splitting of word and world, there is no truth that needs getting at, thus there is no God, for the correspondence of word and world, and the chance to arrive at truth, to my mind at least, assumes a God. The stakes, as our critic writes, are theological.[14] Here may be an instance in which the fundamentalists have the better of the argument, that is, this method, this way of reading texts, appears to be so indissolubly linked to a peculiar worldview that the choice or abandonment of the one involves the choice or abandonment of the other — there is no going at things piecemeal, only at the whole loaf. At any rate, this separation of word from world, this dissolution of the self in favor of "cosmic rhythms to which we must learn to surrender ourselves,"[15] this dismantling of meaning, for

---

13. George Steiner, *Real Presences* (Chicago: University of Chicago Press, 1991), 100.

14. *Real Presences*, 86-87.

15. Iris Murdoch, *Metaphysics as a Guide to Morals* (London: Penguin Books, 1992), 209.

which a myth is as good as a fact, or the false as good as the true — this hides a determinism more frightening than anything in Augustine or Islam.

Finally, there is the matter of engagement, of encounter with the text. The one thing, perhaps the one good thing, remaining to us from a Schlatter, a Barth, or even a Bultmann is that the entire self of the interpreter must be taken captive in interpretation. Most often, that axiom has been applied only with respect to its anthropological side: Apart from the interpreter's goodwill, empathy, or readiness to find truth, understanding cannot occur. But I believe the axiom has far greater validity with regard to the nature of the Bible itself. Current malaise concerning historical-critical method, current flight from interpretation, all that lurching toward analysis, and the ideology that goes with it are, somehow or other, all the work of the Bible itself. It will not be understood, it refuses to be understood solely as an object amenable to laboratory investigation — the indissoluble intertwining of fact and interpretation that gives the historian such headaches is witness to that! It will have a man's or woman's heart and soul, and if not, it will work despair, a summoning up of old ghosts — all that activity that appears so full of confidence but is really only a whistling in the dark. Just as a sonata takes its revenge on someone without an ear for music, so the Scriptures of Old and New Testaments wreak fury on whoever refuses to break with old cognitions, old moralities, who will not be "converted." The evidence for it mounts higher every day, in all that confused prattle of an entire guild of interpreters, amnesiac, and reading only themselves, in a frenzy to tell or hear something new, but emerging only with "the same song, second verse, a little louder, and a little worse." What needs to be done in reclaiming the Bible for the church is not what needs to be done in order to save the Bible, but in order to save the church. Whoever you are, if you do not repent and believe the testimony laid down in this book concerning God and his Christ, it will judge you to inconsequence, render your reading of it, your interpretation of it, your preaching on it a comic spectacle to the world to which you believed you had to adjust it, and your church will die. As well it should.

But whether or not you repent and believe, somewhere, in some corner of it, the world will always take up this Book and read. And in that lies hope. A few years ago, Heinz Cassirer, Oxford don, celebrated son of a celebrated father, at the tender age of fifty got himself a Bible that threw the axiom on which he'd built his whole life and his career in doubt, the axiom that the capacity to act so as to render one's activity a maxim for universal behavior is given at birth. He read in the prophets who convinced him that this could only occur by way of a miracle, and forcing his way through to the New Testament read that this had in fact occurred with Jesus. He got himself baptized, abandoned his university chair, and spent the remainder of his days reading Hebrew and Greek. The Bible does not need saving. It will have its way, because of the word of the God it attests. As I see it, the question before you is whether or not it will have its way with you.

Reclaiming Our Roots and Vision: Scripture and the Stability of the Christian Church

ALISTER E. McGRATH

There are several dangers in using the literary device of parody. One of them is that the parody bears little relation to real life, and is simply a gross distortion of the ways things really are. But there is another danger. The parody may be so close to reality that it alarms us, and forces us to realize that the way things are just cannot be allowed to continue. I believe that if there is any element of parody in what I am about to offer, it comes considerably closer to the second rather than the first of these two dangers. It seems to me that the right of the church to interpret the Bible is treated with contempt by many within the academy. "You are amateurs. You know nothing about reader-orientated criticism. You are not fully acquainted with the *oeuvre* of Michel Foucault. You lack the cool and clinical detachment of the academy. You're biased. We're not."

This comes dangerously close to what Martin Kähler termed "the papacy of the professors" — that is, the unilateral declaration on the part of a self-appointed professional elite that it possesses a monopoly on correct biblical interpretation, which cannot be undertaken without the aid of a gamut of sophisticated techniques that are not available to others outside this charmed circle. Writers in this category use a whole range of subliminal code words like "maturity," "sophistication," and "relevance" to smuggle in an entire value system that is often not made available for public scrutiny, but which often amounts to the simple belief that folk who treat the Bible as having some kind of authority are intellectual relics from the late Stone Age.

The demand for detachment is also highly problematic. As someone who began his academic career as a natural scientist, I am intensely aware of the fact that allegedly neutral "observation" is actually theory laden. What you observe reflects what you expect to see; it is only when there is a serious disjunction between theory and observation that the theory has to be abandoned.[1] Similarly, since Bultmann, we have all learned to wonder if there is any such thing as "presuppositionless exegesis," whether in the academy or the church. The demand for detachment is quite simply an illicit claim to an objectivity that cannot be had in practice. At least the church is honest about this: It interprets Scripture from the standpoint of faith, and has the graciousness to be open about it. But others within the academy allow us to understand that they have access to a privileged standpoint, devoid of any such commitment — when no such privileged standpoint exists in reality.[2]

One of the merits of the kind of postliberal approaches that are emerging from Yale and Duke University Divinity Schools is that they explicitly acknowledge the importance of *tradition* in transmitting values, theories, and outlooks, and move us away from the somewhat naive claims to "detachment" that are found in other academic contexts.[3] I concede that these people may be "detached" in one sense of the word;

1. See Norwood Hanson, *Perception and Discovery: An Introduction to Scientific Inquiry* (San Franciso: Harper, 1969).

2. I explore this issue in more detail in my *Genesis of Doctrine* (Oxford/Cambridge, Mass.: Blackwell, 1990), 90-102, 172-85.

3. See Sheila Greeve Davaney and Delwin Brown, "Postliberalism," in A. E. McGrath, ed., *The Blackwell Encyclopaedia of Modern Christian Thought* (Oxford/Cambridge, Mass.: Blackwell, 1993), 453-56.

they may be indifferent to what they study, and find Scripture unexciting and irrelevant to life. But if they believe that they are detached in the sense of being devoid of precommitments — the kind of thing that the Enlightenment used to call *prejudice* before people realized that the Enlightenment was just as prejudiced as the rest of us[4] — then we must ask some hard questions about whether they are on the same page as the real world.

Anyway, where has this demand for detachment got us? Is it any wonder that there has been a spiralling demand for courses on spirituality in seminaries[5] if we are forced to study Scripture in this way? In response to the suggestion that Scripture "is best studied in cool and clinical detachment," a noted evangelical writer has commented:

> Detachment from *what*, you ask? Why, from the relational activity of trusting, loving, worshipping, obeying, serving and glorifying God: the activity that results from realizing that one is actually in God's presence, actually being addressed by him, every time one opens the Bible or reflects on any divine truth whatsoever.[6]

We need to note the strongly christological dimension of an appeal to Scripture. My distinguished Oxford colleague John Barton has suggested that "Christians are not those who believe in the Bible, but those who believe in Christ."[7] While this has some merit as a statement of priorities and emphases, it seems to me that it sets up a misleading false dichotomy. It is not a question of *either* the Bible *or* Jesus Christ, as if they

---

4. A point stressed by Hans-Georg Gadamer, especially in his *Truth and Method* (London: Sheed and Ward, 1975).

5. See Walter L. Liefield and Linda M. Cannell, "Spiritual Formation and Theological Education," in J. I. Packer and L. Wilkinson, eds., *Alive to God: Studies in Spirituality* (Downers Grove, Ill.: InterVarsity, 1992), 239-52.

6. James I. Packer, "An Introduction to Systematic Spirituality," *Crux* 26 (March 1990): 2-8; quote on p. 6.

7. John Barton, *People of the Book?* (London: SPCK, 1988), 83.

can or should be separated. There is an organic and essential connection between them. We honour Christ by receiving both the Scriptures that he received, and those that the church has handed down to us as a divinely inspired witness to Christ.

Following on from what has just been said, Christology and biblical authority are inextricably linked, in that it is Scripture that brings us to a knowledge of Jesus Christ. At one point, the Genevan reformer John Calvin defined this as the whole point of Scripture.[8] The New Testament is the only document we possess that the Christian church has recognized as authentically embodying and recollecting its understanding of Jesus, and the impact that he had upon people's lives and thoughts. The reports we have concerning Jesus from extracanonical sources are of questionable reliability and of strictly limited value.[9] The same God who gave Jesus Christ also gave Scripture both as a testimony to Christ, and for the community of faith, as a living body that hands down and hands over this knowledge[10] — knowledge in both the cognitive and experiential aspects of that term. It is through Scripture, passed down in and through the witness and worship of the living community of faith, that we, who live after Christ, have access to the living Word of God, given in history.

The relevance of this point would, of course, be disputed by those who argue that Christianity has at best a peripheral or accidental connection with Jesus Christ — for example, those who argue that Christianity should be seen as a set of self-sufficient ideas and values that may have been introduced by Jesus, but that nevertheless retain their validity indepen-

8. *Ioannis Calvini opera quae supersunt omnia*, 59 vols. (Brunschweig/Berlin: Schwetschke, 1863-1900), 9:815, "Mais fault que nostre entendement soit du tout arresté à ce poinct, d'apprendre en l'Escriture à cognoistre Iesus Christ seulement."

9. See David Wenham, ed., *The Jesus Tradition Outside the Gospels* (Sheffield: SOTS, 1984).

10. I take this dynamic process to be the essence of *traditio*, rather than regarding tradition as a static and fixed body of beliefs that results from such a process.

dently of his person or work. A sharp distinction is thus drawn between the historical person of Jesus Christ and the universally valid principles that he is alleged to transmit, embody, or represent — principles that owe their validity to criteria other than being grounded in the history of Jesus.

However, the plausibility of this viewpoint is increasingly being questioned, both on empirical and theoretical grounds. There is growing sympathy for the traditional insistence that Christianity is grounded in and focussed upon the person and work of Jesus Christ. Once this point is conceded, in whole or part, the centrality of Scripture to Christian doctrine, worship, and spirituality will be clear. It will also be clear that Scripture is thus seen as a means, rather than an end. Scripture is read in order to encounter Christ; it is like a lens through which Christ is brought into focus. It was Martin Luther who declared that "Scripture is the manger in which Christ is laid." More formally, Karl Barth has argued that

> When Holy Scripture speaks of God, it does not permit us to let our attention or thoughts wander at random. . . . When Holy Scripture speaks of God, it concentrates our attention and thoughts upon one single point and what is to be known at that point. . . . If we ask further concerning the one point upon which, according to Scripture, our attention and thoughts should and must be concentrated, then from first to last the Bible directs us to the name of Jesus Christ.[11]

Within my own Anglican tradition, the same point was made by a former Archbishop of Canterbury, Arthur Michael Ramsey, who declared that "the importance of the confession 'Jesus is Lord' is not only that Jesus is divine but that God is Christlike."[12]

11. Karl Barth, *Church Dogmatics*, 14 vols. (Edinburgh: Clark, 1936-75), II/2: 52-53.
12. Arthur Michael Ramsey, *God, Christ and the World* (London: SCM Press, 1969), 98.

ALISTER E. McGRATH

The authority of Scripture thus rests upon both theological and historical considerations; it is through Jesus Christ that the distinctively Christian knowledge of God comes about, and this knowledge of Jesus is given only in Scripture. Christ is what gives Scripture its unity; as Stephen Neill, among many others, has emphasized, the central thought and subject that binds all parts of the Bible together, and in the light of which they are to be interpreted, is the person and work of Jesus Christ.[13]

The role of Scripture in public worship is also of importance. We need to be reminded that Scripture is to be read with a sense of *expectation and anticipation*. The liturgical affirmation that Scripture is "the word of the Lord," common to many mainline churches, declares that the public reading of Scripture is to be revered and honored as a God-given means of grace. There is an intimate and organic connection between the church and Scripture that, it seems to me, ultimately defies simple classification in terms of the priority of church over Scripture, or Scripture over the church.

The issue of authority is important here. Despite the widespread recognition of the demise of the Enlightenment, its emphasis upon individual autonomy remains as powerful as ever. True, autonomy is no longer generally grounded in the universal truths of reason, to which individual thinkers have access, but in the right of individuals to construct their own private world as they think fit. The suggestion that some external norm must be taken into account, or that it may have a controlling influence over our thought is regarded with suspicion. Reclaiming Scripture for the church involves recognizing that this text has its own voice, which may refuse to passively acquiesce to our own whims and predilections, and may force us to reappraise our understanding of the nature of Christianity.

13. Stephen Neill, *The Supremacy of Jesus* (London: Hodder & Stoughton, 1984), 9-17. Perhaps his finest popular exploration of this theme is to be found in *The Challenge of Jesus Christ* (Madras: SPCK India, 1944).

Yet this does not for one moment imply that the Bible has an alien and imposed authority over the community of faith. On the basis of any reasonable analysis of the process of the formation of the canon of the New Testament, it may be argued that the community of faith *chose* to recognize the New Testament as authoritative. This is widely regarded as an acknowledgment both of the need for such authority, and of the natural authority that the individual components of the New Testament were already exercising within the church.

The Babylonian Captivity of Scripture

I have deliberately borrowed Luther's 1520 image of the "Babylonian captivity of the church" to make the point that the study of Scripture has become exiled from its homeland. Formerly undertaken within the community of faith, it has been banished to a community with its own definite — although often unacknowledged and unstated — sets of beliefs and values. As a result, it is held in bondage. It is not free to challenge those beliefs, but is judged in their light. We have all learned to realize that the interpretation of Scripture serves the power needs of the interpreter; this maxim, sadly, applies as much to the academic community as the church. Scripture has thus become subservient to the needs and requirements of a fragmented academic community, in which originality and innovation are valued, and "faithfulness to a tradition" is regarded as derivative, tedious, and tantamount to some kind of intellectual fascism.

But I also use the image of the "Babylonian captivity of the church" to suggest that a return from that exile is possible. As the history of Israel reminds us, there will be those who will be happy to remain in exile, living among their captors. But my suggestion is that the possibility of a homecoming, of a return, is both real and realistic. There is growing awareness that the interpretation of Scripture has its proper place within the community of faith, which recognizes in the Bible far more than a historical narrative. The reading of the Bible in the public worship of the Christian community is an important affirmation of both the kerygmatic and didactic role of Scripture in generating, nourishing, and guiding faith.[14]

Critics of the notion of biblical authority sometimes suggest that we would be liberated if we were to abandon the authority of Scripture. It seems to me that this is nonsense, and merely opens the door to being forced to acknowledge the authority of something — or someone — else. The Christian insistence upon the authority of Scripture reflects a determination not to permit anything from outside the Christian heritage to become the norm for what is truly "Christian." Theological history has provided us with many all too uncomfortable examples of what happens when a theology cuts itself loose from the controlling influence of the Christian tradition, and seeks norms from outside that tradition.

There is no difficulty about providing examples of the manner in which Christian thought has become captive to a prevailing ideology. A classic example is provided by the "imperial theology," whose formulation is especially associated with Eusebius of Caesarea, which shackled the exposition of Scripture (especially its messianic passages) to an ideology that saw the Roman empire as the climax of God's redemptive purposes. With the conversion of the Roman emperor Constantine in the fourth century, a new era in Christian history had dawned. Some Christian writers, most notably Eusebius, portrayed Constantine as an instrument chosen by God for the conversion of the empire. Eusebius's "Rome-theology" appears to have had a deep impact upon Christian thinking in this crucial period, not least in rendering Rome virtually immune from reflective criticism on the part of Christian writers.

Indeed, so intimate was the connection that came to be presupposed between empire and gospel that the sack of Rome

14. On such points, see Darrell Jodock, "The Reciprocity Between Scripture and Theology: The Role of Scripture in Contemporary Theological Reflection," *Interpretation* 44 (1990): 369-82.

(410) came dangerously close to precipitating the end of Christianity itself. The fall of Rome raised a series of potentially difficult questions for the imperial theology. Why had Rome been sacked? Augustine addresses such questions in *The City of God*, partly to discredit a "theology of history" that had become influential in Christian circles, and liberate Christianity from this straitjacket which had been imposed upon it. The *City of God* topples Rome from its position in Eusebius's theology of history. No longer is Rome portrayed as God's chosen instrument for the salvation of the world and the preservation of the gospel. The restrictive (and highly distorting) controlling influence of an imperial ideology upon the Christian exposition of Scripture was thus removed.[15] As a result, the fall of Rome did not entail the fall of the gospel itself. By enslaving itself to a prevailing ideology, the dominant form of Christian thought had ensured its survival — indeed, its ascendancy — in the short term. But when that ideology collapsed, it brought its allies down with it. At least a substantial section of Christian theology had come to depend upon this ideology. Augustine's great contribution was to allow it to rediscover its true legitimation and foundation in Scripture, as read and received within the church.

A more recent example of such a nonbiblical controlling influence upon Christianity may be found by looking at the history of the German church, which, under Adolf Hitler, was obliged to acknowledge the authority of "German culture." Some meekly submitted to this ideological straitjacket; others were bold enough to insist that Christianity must remain faithful to itself by taking its heritage with the utmost seriousness, and refuse to be controlled by anything other than the living Christ, as we find him in Scripture — a belief stated with electrifying directness in the Barmen Declaration (1934):

15. On this, see R. A. Markus, *Saeculum: History and Society in the Theology of St. Augustine* (Cambridge: Cambridge University Press, 1970); Jaroslav Pelikan, *The Mystery of Continuity: Time and History, Memory and Eternity in the Thought of St. Augustine* (Charlottesville, VA: University of Virginia Press, 1986).

> Jesus Christ, as he is attested for us in Holy Scripture, is the
> one Word of God which we have to hear and which we have
> to trust and obey in life and in death. We reject the false
> doctrine, that the Church could and would have to acknowl-
> edge as a source of its proclamation, apart from and besides
> this one Word of God, still other events and powers, figures
> and truths, as God's revelation.[16]

There is a lesson here for today's Western churches, who often
seem to be throwing themselves uncritically at the feet of
today's cultural norms. Only by rediscovering norms outside
and apart from our culture may we avoid becoming enslaved
to what Alasdair MacIntyre has styled the "Self-Images of the
Age." We criticize the German Christians for obeying Hitler,
conveniently choosing to overlook that they were simply sub-
mitting themselves to the prevailing cultural norms. We are
doing the same today by allowing ourselves and our churches
to follow societal norms and values, irrespective of their
origins and goals. To allow our ideas and values to become
controlled by anything or anyone other than the self-revelation
of God in Scripture is to adopt an ideology rather than a
theology; it is to become controlled by ideas and values whose
origins lie outside the Christian tradition — and potentially to
become enslaved to them.

Such ideas and values may be powerful correctives to lazy
and irresponsible theologies, just as Marxism has provided an
overdue critique of Christian social thought, and feminism of
patriarchal tendencies within the church. But Marxist values
and "women's experience" — to name but two pertinent examples to which others could readily be added — cannot become *foundational* for Christianity, which is grounded in God,
as known in Christ. The example of the German church under
Hitler is instructive, in that it points to the need for a criterion
by which the church can judge the secular world. A theology

16. Arthur Cochrane, ed., *Reformed Confessions of the Sixteenth Century*
(London: SCM Press, 1966), 334.

that is grounded in values, whether radical or conservative, drawn solely from the secular world becomes powerless to criticize that world. If your ideas are grounded in a set of beliefs or values, you are hardly in a position to criticize them — you would just be pulling the rug from under your own feet. A theology grounded in German culture thus found itself without any credible means to criticize that culture when it turned nasty. What was once believed to be liberating turned out to be decidedly menacing and sinister. It is significant that it was theologians such as Karl Barth and Dietrich Bonhoeffer, who refused to look for God anywhere other than in Jesus Christ, who provided the most serious and thoughtful opposition in the culture wars waged by the Third Reich.

To illustrate how Scripture can be enslaved by those who profess to liberate it, I shall explore the writings of John Shelby Spong, especially his *Rescuing the Bible from Fundamentalism* (1991).[17] All of us know about the problem of fundamentalism. In 1910, the first of a series of twelve books entitled *The Fundamentals* appeared.[18] By a series of historical accidents, the term "fundamentalist" took its name from this series of works. Fundamentalism arose as a religious reaction within American culture to the rise of a secular culture.[19] Despite the wide use of the term to refer to religious movements within Islam and Judaism, the term originally and properly designates a movement within Protestant Christianity in the United States, especially during the period 1920 to 1940. The weaknesses of this movement are well known, and do not require documentation here. But if we are to reject fundamentalism, what are we to replace it with? There is a real need to rescue the Bible from fundamentalism; but those who claim to rescue it often shackle it to their own ends.

17. John Shelby Spong, *Rescuing the Bible from Fundamentalism* (San Francisco: HarperCollins, 1991).

18. *The Fundamentals: A Testimony of the Truth*, 12 vols. (Chicago: Testimony Publishing Company, 1910-15).

19. The definitive study remains George Marsden, *Fundamentalism and American Culture: The Shaping of Twentieth Century Evangelicalism 1870-1925* (New York: Oxford University Press, 1980).

73

And this is where Bishop Spong, a maverick bishop with a genius for self-publicization, comes in. In his *Rescuing the Bible from Fundamentalism* — a work that would probably have been dismissed as utterly inconsequential were its writer not a bishop (a fact heavily emphasized on its front cover) — Spong offers to liberate the Bible from a fundamentalist stranglehold. But it soon becomes clear that the Bible is to be "liberated" only to be enslaved to the latest cultural norms prevailing among the greater New England liberal elite. This work is as aggressive in its modernity as it is selective and superficial in its argumentation and intolerant and dismissive of the views of others. For example, at one point Spong tentatively advances the idea that Paul might have been a homosexual. A few pages later, this seems to have become an established result of New Testament scholarship, leading Spong to the conclusion that one of the church's greatest teachers was a "rigidly controlled gay male."[20] The hard historical evidence for this dramatic assertion? Nil. One cannot help wondering if the New Testament is being less than subtly massaged here, to fit the sensitivities of a retrospective liberal conscience.

Much the same thing can be seen in his *Born of a Woman* (1992),[21] in which we learn that Mary, far from being a virgin, was actually a rape victim. The hard historical evidence for this? Nil. Yet Spong apparently expects his readers to take his views on board as the assured findings of New Testament scholarship, and reconstruct their vision of the Christian faith and life as a result. One cannot help but feel that reasoned argumentation has here been replaced by a special pleading and petulant assertion, more characteristic of the fundamentalist groups to which Bishop Spong takes such exception.

Bishop Spong recognizes that his views are unpopular, and believes that this is because they are thoroughly up-to-date and intellectually respectable. Sadly, they are just unpopular.

20. Spong, *Rescuing the Bible from Fundamentalism*, 108-25.
21. John Shelby Spong, *Born of a Woman: A Bishop Rethinks the Birth of Jesus* (San Francisco: HarperCollins, 1992).

Spong constructs a fantasy world in which his own vision of a politically correct culture leads him to impose political and social stereotypes upon the New Testament with a fierce and uncritical dogmatism and a lack of scholarly insight and responsibility that many had assumed were only associated with the likes of Jerry Falwell. The pseudo-scholarly character of Spong's approach has been pointed out by N. T. Wright.[22] Commenting on Spong's attempts to cast himself as a persecuted hero, standing for the truth in the midst of a fundamentalist ocean, Wright remarks:

> [Spong] rushes on, constructing imaginary historical worlds and inviting us to base our faith and life upon them. If we refuse this invitation he will, no doubt, hurl his favourite abuse-word at us again. But if everyone who disagrees with Spong's book turns out to be a fundamentalist, then I suppose that all the fundamentalist churches in the world would not be able to contain the new members who would suddenly arrive on their doorsteps.[23]

My point is that it is not enough to argue for the need to wrest Scripture free from those who imprison it within the severe limitations of a fundamentalist approach. Too often, the professed liberators of Scripture proceed immediately to imprison it within their own worldview. This is no liberation; this is merely a change in dictators, similar to that experienced by those unfortunate enough to live in the eastern regions of Germany in 1945, who found themselves liberated from Hitler only to discover that they had been rescued by Stalin.

22. N. T. Wright, *Who Was Jesus?* (Grand Rapids: Eerdmans, 1992), 65-92. Wright himself is in the process of writing a major five-volume study of the historical and theological questions surrounding the origins of Christianity, of which the first has now appeared: *The New Testament and the People of God* (Minneapolis: Fortress Press, 1992). This work will be of fundamental importance to an informed and reponsible understanding of the issues treated so superficially by Spong.

23. Wright, *Who Was Jesus?* 91-92.

There is an urgent need to regain the center; to reform a central position that avoids the absurdities and inadequacies of the fundamentalist and liberal positions. I concede that both these approaches were, in their original forms, sincere and well-motivated attempts to relate the gospel to modern culture. But both have failed — one by refusing to pay any attention to modern culture and urging a retreat behind it, the other by allowing itself to be overwhelmed by it. We must forge an environment in which Scripture is honored and revered and allowed to challenge our preconceptions and values, forcing us to inquire where our ideas actually come from. We need to establish a context for the reading and study of Scripture that recognizes an organic connection between this text and the community that gathers around it, and relates directly to the events, ideas, values, and experiences that it relates and commends. Yet this community and environment does not need to be *invented*. It is already there, in the worshipping community of the church. Our task is to rediscover, retrieve, and recollect — not to begin all over again.

Theological liberalism has asked us to seek norms drawn from human experience and culture, and acknowledge the authority of Scripture where it happens to endorse or resonate with these. The difficulty for liberalism is that its cultural accommodationism simply makes Christian theology a hostage to the dominant cultural ideology, in a manner that shows alarming parallels with the situation that developed in the German Church crisis of the mid-1930s.[24] The Barmen Declaration was not only a protest against Hitler and Nazism (though that it unquestionably was); it also represented a passionate affirmation of the need for Christian faith and the-

---

24. See the disquieting analysis by Robert P. Ericksen, *Theologians under Hitler: Gerhard Kittel, Paul Althaus, and Emanuel Hirsch* (New Haven: Yale University Press, 1985). The case of Emanuel Hirsch (1888-1972), who openly supported the Nazis, is especially significant. For further documentation, see the series *Arbeiten zur Geschichte des Kirchenkampfes* (Göttingen and Zürich: Vandenhoeck & Ruprecht, n.d.).

ology to avoid entangling themselves in the bonds of a prevailing culture. As Stanley Hauerwas and William H. Willimon comment:

> For Barth, and for us, Nazi Germany was the supreme test for modern theology. There we experienced the "modern world," which we had so labored to understand and to become credible to, as the world, not only of the Copernican world view, computers, and the dynamo, but also of the Nazis. Barth was horrified that his church lacked the theological resources to stand against Hitler. It was the theological liberals, those who had spent their theological careers translating the faith into terms that could be understood by modern people, and used in the creation of modern civilization, who were unable to say no. Some, like Emanuel Hirsch, even said yes to Hitler.[25]

Hirsch, like so many other German liberal theologians at the time, was unable to discern the dangers of allowing theology to slide into bondage to the prevailing culture — even when that culture became Nazi.

It should also be recalled here that it was the German academics who lent their full support to the war policy of Kaiser Wilhelm in 1914.[26] And what, one wonders, was the Soviet academy doing throughout the dark night of the Russian soul? All the evidence points to Soviet academics being little more than puppets who lent covert support to the shocking oppression of Stalinism. It is often suggested that the academy is the safeguarder of liberty. The evidence does not endorse this. The church must look elsewhere than to the academy, and above all to her own distinctive identity and

25. Stanley Hauerwas and William H. Willimon, *Resident Aliens: Life in the Christian Colony* (Nashville: Abingdon Press, 1989), 24-25.

26. Wilfried Härle, "Der Aufruf der 93 Intellektuellen und Karl Barths Bruch mit der liberalen Theologie," *Zeitschrift für Theologie und Kirche* 72 (1975): 207-24.

resources, if she is to maintain her liberty and avoid perennial exile on the edge of a secular culture.

Reclaiming the Bible for the church is thus something profoundly liberating. It frees us from the slavish demand that we follow every cultural trend, and offers us a framework whereby we may *judge* them, as the Confessing Church chose to judge Hitler rather than follow him — despite the enormous cultural pressure placed upon them to conform to the prevailing cultural climate. Reclaiming the Bible allows us to imitate Christ rather than the latest whim of a fragmented and confused culture.[27]

Rooted in Scripture:
Rediscovering Christian Identity

I now want to offer a specifically European perspective on our theme, which I think is helpful in setting things in a broader context. (In offering this perspective, I assume it will be obvious that I am not indulging in Eurocentrism. I am merely pointing out how what has been happening in one cultural situation may cast light on what is happening in another.) A major development in European culture since the collapse of Marxism in Eastern Europe since 1989 has been the rediscovery of national identity in the region. Peoples who had been forced to conform to the same faceless and monolithic identity of artificial political entities — such as the Soviet Union and Yugoslavia — have reacted against this imposition of uniformity, and reasserted their distinctive identities. Russia, the Ukraine, Lithuania, Slovenia, and Croatia are among the nations that have reemerged as distinct entities

27. Further documentation of this point is impossible within the space available. The kind of approach I would be inclined to follow is mapped out in Alister E. McGrath, "Christian Ethics," in *The Religion of the Incarnation: Anglican Essays in Commemoration of Lux Mundi* (Bristol: Bristol Classic Press, 1989), 189-204.

in recent years — entities that are proud of their distinctiveness.

The political dimensions of this development are obvious. After a period of enforced conformity to an abstract universal, for which they felt no affinity or affection, national and cultural groups are once more free to affirm and embrace their distinctive identities. They have often done so with a degree of enthusiasm, triumphalism, and aggressiveness that has alarmed many observers. This development has strongly religious overtones, as the revival of Christianity in Eastern Europe and Islam in the southeastern republics of the former Soviet Union has demonstrated. In making this observation, I am in no way condoning violence or militant nationalism. I am simply pointing out what happens when people's distinctive identities are trampled underfoot and devalued. The denial of distinctiveness creates an atmosphere of oppression that is a fertile breeding ground for militarism, extremism, and revolt. Distinctiveness matters, and must be respected.

In the West, we are seeing a related development, through the collapse of the credibility and plausibility of a liberal worldview. At the height of its influence, theological liberalism behaved rather like Marxism in Eastern Europe. Differences between the religions were ruthlessly suppressed, in the name of what George Lindbeck has termed "homogenization." Despite other worthy claimants to the title, the high priest of this cult is widely regarded as being John Hick. All religions, we are told, are saying the same thing. They are foolish and arrogant enough to believe that they are different; in reality, they are merely offering different perspectives on the same things — or, more accurately, the same "ultimate reality."

On the basis of this theory, Hick has embarked on a comprehensive program to eliminate anything distinctive within Christianity. The doctrine of the incarnation is dismissed as a myth. But why? In a recent critique of the christological views of John Hick, Pannenberg points out that "Hick's proposal of religious pluralism as an option of authentically Christian theology hinges on the condition of a prior demolition of the traditional doctrine of the incarnation." Hick, Pannenberg notes, assumes that this demolition has already taken place, and chides him for his excessive selectivity — not to mention his lack of familiarity with recent German theology! — in drawing such a conclusion.[28] Hick also dismisses the resurrection of Jesus, apparently alarmed at the impact that such a distinctive and unique doctrine might have on his homogenizing worldview.

A similar note is struck in relation to the doctrine of the Trinity. The loose and vague talk about "God" or "Ultimate Reality" found in much pluralist writing is not a result of theological sloppiness or confusion. It is a considered response to the recognition that for Christians to talk about the Trinity is to speak about a specific God (not just "deity" in general), who has chosen to be known in and through Jesus Christ. As Robert Jenson has persuasively argued, the doctrine of the Trinity is an attempt to spell out the identity of this God, and to avoid confusion with rival claimants to this title.[29] The doctrine of the Trinity defines and defends the distinctiveness — indeed, the *uniqueness* — of the "God of the Christians." The New Testament gives a further twist to this development through its language about "the God and Father of our Lord Jesus Christ," locating the identity of God in the actions and passion of Jesus Christ. To put it bluntly: God is christologically disclosed.

In an important recent study, Kathryn Tanner makes the point that liberal pluralist theology has succumbed to "colonialist discourse."[30] The crude pluralist attempt to reduce religions to manifestations of the same transcendental impulses, or to minimize their differences for the sake of theoretical neatness, is totally unacceptable:

28. Wolfhart Pannenberg, "Religious Pluralism and Conflicting Truth Claims," in G. D'Costa, ed., *Christian Uniqueness Reconsidered* (Maryknoll, New York: Orbis, 1990), 96-106, quote on 100.

29. Robert Jenson, *The Triune Identity* (Philadelphia: Fortress Press, 1982), 1-20.

30. Kathyrn Tanner, "Respect for Other Religions: A Christian Antidote to Colonialist Discourse," *Modern Theology* 9 (1993): 1-18.

Pluralist generalizations about what all religions have in common conflict with genuine dialogue, in that they prejudge its results. Commonalities, which should be established in and through a process of dialogue, are constructed ahead of time by pluralists to serve as presuppositions of dialogue. Pluralists therefore close themselves to what people of other religions might have to say about their account of these commonalities. Moreover, . . . a pluralist focus on commonalities slights differences among the religions of the world. The pluralists' insistence on commonalities as a condition of dialogue shows an unwillingness to recognize the depth and degree of diversity among religions, or the positive importance of them.[31]

In addition, Tanner makes the point that pluralists conceal the "particularities of their own perspectives by claiming to form generalizations about the religions of the world." Apart from being untrue, Tanner remarks, this approach "brings pluralist theorists of religion close to the kind of absolutism that it is part of their own project to avoid."[32]

But the hegemony of liberalism is over. The embargo on being different has been lifted. Christianity is free to be itself once more, liberated from the stifling paternalism of a "we're all saying the same thing, really" worldview — a worldview that, I may add, was found just as nauseating by non-Christians as it was by Christians. We are free to rediscover our distinctive identity as Christians in this world. And how are we to do that? By returning to our roots. By rediscovering that we are different. And reclaiming Scripture as the common heritage of all Christian believers is an integral element of this great process of coming to life once more, now that the homogenizing iron curtain has been lifted.

In their magisterial survey of recent trends in mainline

31. Tanner, "Respect for Other Religions," 2.
32. Tanner, "Respect for Other Religions," 2. See also John Apczynski, "John Hick's Theocentrism: Revolution or Implicitly Exclusive?" *Modern Theology* 8 (1992): 39-52.

American religion, Wade Clark Roof and William McKinney demonstrate how the shift toward inclusiveness and the need to be seen to be "relevant" to an increasingly secular American culture have led to the steady erosion of distinctiveness on the part of the mainline Christian churches.

> A crucial challenge for liberal Protestantism is to recapture some sense of particularity as a community of memory, and not merely as a custodian of generalized cultural values. This will require among other things a countering of the secular drift that has had a disproportionate impact on its traditional constituency.[33]

Theology concerns the quest for justifiable particularity. For some, this suggestion will seem arrogant and imperialist. Yet, in fairness it must be pointed out that such criticisms pre-empt any individuals or bodies from laying claim to any distinctive positions whatsoever, lest they be accused of elitism. To be different is not to be superior; it is just to be different. The liberal trend toward homogenization — "we're all saying the same thing" — eliminates the diversity of life in favor of a dull grey monochrome, where none is allowed to be different. But Christianity *is* distinct. After all, Jesus Christ was not crucified just for reinforcing what everyone already knew. With the end of the Enlightenment, the embargo on distintinctiveness has been lifted. No longer is the claim to be saying something *different* seen as equivalent to being irrational. Jews are special; they have a special story and a different set of values. In the same way, Christians are special; they have a special story and a different set of values.[34] It is perhaps here that liberalism has most failed the church, and contributed to its sense of lack of purpose.

To reclaim Scripture for the church is to lay claim to

---

33. Wade Clark Roof and William McKinney, *American Mainline Religion: Its Changing Shape and Future* (New Brunswick, NJ: Rutgers University Press, 1987), 241.

34. Hauerwas and Willimon, *Resident Aliens*, 18.

rediscovering and reappropriating our roots. The church is a "Scripture-Shaped Community," to use a helpful phrase of Richard B. Hays.[35] The history of Western European culture has been deeply affected by the search for roots. Cultural stability and enrichment have often been seen as inextricably linked. This is perhaps most clearly seen in the case of the Italian Renaissance, rightly regarded as one of the most important and creative periods in Western culture. The art galleries and museums of the world are packed full of exhibits showing the remarkable originality and imagination of the new culture that took hold of northern Italy during the period 1350 to 1550. By the end of the sixteenth century, virtually all of Western Europe had been infected by this astonishing enthusiasm and vision. But what lay behind this magnificent outburst of energy, of incredible artistic excitement, at the time?

The answer to this question is complex. However, a substantial part of that answer can be stated in two Latin words: "*ad fontes*, back to the original sources." Italian culture gained a new sense of purpose and dignity by seeing itself as the modern heir and champion of the long-dead culture of classical Rome. The Italian Renaissance could be said to be about bringing the culture of ancient Rome back to life in the modern period. The imaginations of artists, architects, poets, writers, and theologians were seized by this vision. Imagine being able to allow the glory of the past to interact with the cultural void of fourteenth-century Italy! And as the process of recollection of cultural roots began, Italy began to gain a reputation as the center of a new civilization in Europe.

It is thus no accident that Italy was the birthplace and cradle of the Renaissance. The Italian writers of the period appear to have seen themselves as returning to their cultural roots, in the world of classical Rome.[36] A stream, they argued,

---

35. Richard B. Hays, "Scripture-Shaped Community: The Problem of Method in New Testament Ethics," *Interpretation* 44 (1990): 42-55.

36. Roberto Weiss, *The Renaissance Discovery of Classical Antiquity* (Oxford: Blackwell, 1988). For further documentation, see Alister E. McGrath,

was purest at its source; why not return to that source, instead of being satisfied with the muddy and stagnant waters of existing medieval culture? The past was seen as a resource, a foundational influence, whose greatness demanded that it should be allowed a voice in the present. The Italian Renaissance arose through a decision to allow the historic roots of Italian culture to impose upon the present, to inform it, to stimulate it — and to transform it. The explosion of creativity that resulted is an eloquent and powerful witness to the potential effects of returning to cultural roots and allowing them to impact upon the present.

Western Christianity has been deeply affected by this concern for roots. In differing ways, both the sixteenth-century Reformation and the nineteenth-century Oxford Movement represented a systematic attempt to return to the vision of the New Testament or apostolic church. One of the central insights that binds Christians from many denominational backgrounds together is the realization that the church of today needs to be constantly challenged and nourished by returning to its roots in the apostolic era. This is no historical romanticism, based on the belief that things were better in the past than they now are. Rather, it is the realization that the church needs to be reminded of its reason for being there in the first place, if it is ever to regain its sense of mission and purpose in the world. Just as the Renaissance led to an enrichment of European culture by a return to its sources, so the life and witness of the modern church can be enriched and nourished by a constant return to its sources in the New Testament. Here is a fundamental reason for reclaiming Scripture for the church — the need to secure our identity. While this trend would be vigorously resisted by those who insist that Christianity is not distinctive, that viewpoint has had its day.

The Intellectual Origins of the European Reformation (Oxford/Cambridge, MA: Blackwell, 1987).

At first sight, this respect for roots might seem to be a recipe for a reactionary mind-set, encouraging unoriginality and the stifling of creativity. That danger must be conceded. But there is another side to this story. Commitment to a tradition is not equivalent to an encrusted dogmatism, a denial of the freedom to think, or of the importance of creativity.[37] To take Scripture seriously is to allow the past to speak to us before turning, with a renewed and informed mind, to face the issues of the present.[38] Freedom to think without an accompanying commitment to a tradition can lead to little more than an unanchored chaos.

The twentieth century has provided us with ample historical examples of what happens when a society breaks free from the restraining force of tradition. Nazi Germany and the Stalinist Soviet Union are excellent illustrations of the unacceptable consequences of a break with tradition. Walter Benjamin's "Theses on the Philosophy of History" reflect his despair at the totalitarianism that results when a civilized society chooses to break with its traditional values.[39] It is very easy to break with one's roots; but, as the cultural history of the former Soviet Union in recent years makes clear, it is very difficult to pick up those roots, once broken. David Tracy is one of many recent writers within a more liberal tradition to express concern over "the wasteful and complacent obstruction of the rich resources of the tradition."[40] Reclaiming Scripture for the church is one vital means by which Christian distinctiveness can be preserved.

37. A point stressed by Jaroslav Pelikan, *The Vindication of Tradition* (New Haven: Yale University Press, 1984).

38. See the suggestive study of Aidan Nichols, "T. S. Eliot and Yves Congar on the Nature of Tradition," *Angelicum* 61 (1984): 473-85, which shows how "tradition" and "originality" are mutually linked.

39. For analysis and comment, see McGrath, *The Genesis of Doctrine*, 165-71.

40. David Tracy, "On Naming the Present," in P. Hillyer, ed., *On the Threshold of the Third Millennium*, Concilium 1990/1 (London: SCM Press, 1990), 66-85; quote on p. 75.

Reclaiming the Bible for the church gives us a basis and foundation on which we may address the world, without being forced simply to echo its words and values. In the midst of a rapidly changing culture, we need stability. And culture itself cannot provide that stability. Nowadays, any theology that rests on cultural norms will find itself becoming obselete before anyone has time to fully figure out what it was saying in the first place. As Peter L. Berger, one of North America's most distinguished sociologists, comments:

> Each time that one has, after an enormous effort, managed to adjust the faith to the prevailing culture, that culture turns around and changes. . . . Our pluralistic culture forces those who would "update" Christianity into a state of permanent nervousness. The "wisdom of the world," which is the standard by which they would modify the religious tradition, varies from one social location to another; what is worse, even in the same locale it keeps on changing, often rapidly.[41]

Berger's sociological analysis makes it clear that some views will be "the accepted wisdom in one social milieu and utter foolishness in another." Or, to put it another way, it is not a universal way of thinking or set of values; it is socially located, in a specific class or social group. It is meaningless to talk about "making Christianity relevant to the modern world," as it presupposes a universality to "the modern world" that is absent in reality. Every attempt to accommodate Christianity to the beliefs of one social grouping proves to make it irrelevant to another. The paradox underlying the entire liberal enterprise is that for everyone for whom the gospel is made "relevant," there is someone else for whom it is made irrelevant. The church simply cannot afford to allow its identity and proclamation to be dictated by such short-term cultural trends, re-

41. Peter L. Berger, *A Far Glory: The Quest for Faith in an Age of Credulity* (New York: Free Press, 1992), 10-11.

stricted to specific sections of society. Reclaiming the Bible is about reclaiming our history, our story, our memories, and our message, in the firm knowledge that we have something to say which the world needs to hear, and are not simply echoing its own voice.

In the recent past, we have been overwhelmed by the force of a rhetoric that has sought to persuade us that there are no other options than an obscurantist fundamentalism and a culturally and intellectually sophisticated liberalism. But that viewpoint now seems to belong to a different world — a world that is now definitely located in the past. The rise of postliberalism and postmodernism symbolize — even if they do not resolve — the collapse of confidence in these certainties of yesteryear. We can now begin to work toward the reconstruction and retrieval of our heritage, by reclaiming the Bible for the church.

In this essay, I have tried to point to some of the considerations that lead me to believe that there is an urgent need to rescue the Bible from its Babylonian captivity. I have had space only to hint at the importance of some of these factors. Let me make it absolutely clear that I have no intention of demanding an embargo on the academic study of Scripture; we need to listen to the critical perspectives of outsiders.[42] Nor do I in any way underestimate the difficulties that lie in our path. What I am demanding is that the Christian community of faith should be recognized as having a right to read and interpret Scripture in its own manner and for its own purposes. As Karl Barth once put it:

> Theology is not a private subject for theologians only. Nor is it a private subject for professors. Fortunately, there have

42. See the outstanding essay of Anthony C. Thiselton, "Academic Freedom, Religious Tradition, and the Morality of Christian Scholarship," in M. Santer, ed., *Their Lord and Ours: Approaches to Authority, Community and the Unity of the Church* (London: SPCK, 1982), 20-45.

always been pastors who understood more about theology than most professors. Nor is theology a private subject of study for pastors. . . . Theology is a matter for the church.[43]

For Christians, the Bible is our book. It tells our story. It judges us, encourages us, and builds us up. Why should we allow others to hijack it?

43. Karl Barth, "Theology," in *God in Action* (Edinburgh: Clark, 1936), 39-57; quote on pp. 56-57.

Hermeneutics and the
Life of the Church

ROBERT W. JENSON

I

The first thing I must do is note the oddity of the church's having to "reclaim" the Bible. For the Bible exists only within the church. Clarity about that will be fundamental to everything that follows.

The volume we call the Bible is a collection of documents. The *single book* exists because the church in her specific mission assembled a certain selection of documents from the very ancient Near East and from first-century Mediterranean antiquity.

Saying this, I mean something commonsensical, that should not ignite theological argument. Protestantism emphasizes that these precise documents *impose* themselves on the church; Catholicism East and West emphasizes that it is the *church* that recognizes the exigency. I mean only to make the simple point presupposed by and included in both emphases: the collection comes together in and for the church.

Where the church's calling to speak the gospel is not shared, the binding of these particular documents between one cover becomes a historical accident of no hermeneutical sig-

nificance. The drastically misnamed Society for Biblical Literature is not essentially more interested in the documents in the
canon than in similar documents outside the canon. For them,
the formation of the canon was the project of an ancient religious movement, through which these valuable objects of historical research and opportunities for hermeneutical virtuosity
were luckily preserved for scholarly ex-Christians from which
to make a living.

Therefore when folk who do not follow the gospel turn
their attention to the Bible, the one book immediately disinte-
grates into its component parts, splitting first into Hebrew
Scripture and New Testament and then into traditions, redactions, and so forth — to which fragments the heathen may be
entirely welcome.

II

So how *is* the church to claim and read the Bible?

The primary hermeneutical principle for the church's
reading of Scripture is — I want to insist — simply the
church's own life. What primarily opens the Bible and guides
the church's reading of it is the churchly life of which biblical
exegesis is itself a part. What God uses to guide our reading
of the Bible is first and foremost the church's liturgy and devotion and catechesis and homiletics, as Scripture has its particular place in them.

So — leaping right in — the Scriptures live and have their
churchly meaning within the church's *liturgy*. We are gathered
here from many ecclesial traditions. But we all practice liturgy
— though some of us may for good or bad reason not like to call
it that — and we all do this within a liturgical tradition. That is,
we all belong to congregations that gather for prayer and praise
and proclamation, both verbal and embodied, and that have
done so for a long time. In all our liturgical traditions, Scripture
has two roles: reading from Scripture is itself an essential liturgical act, and Scripture's language and literary forms and stories

and sayings pervade everything else that is done or said. If our liturgy accurately and richly enacts the *gospel*, then within it, Scripture will say to us what God intends it to say. But if we make up liturgies according to other criteria, to attract the baby-boomers, play off factions in the worship committee or whatever, Scripture captive in such liturgies will *not* say what God intends it to say — and if God *does* use Scripture to speak in these circumstances, it will not say anything we want to hear.

The Scriptures live and have their churchly meaning within the church's *devotion*. "Spirituality" is very big these days, and folk in the church cultivate an astonishing variety of meditative practices. The church's tradition of meditation, however, has been specific. Like other traditions of meditation, Christian meditation begins by emptying the mind; it does not, however, do this for the sake of emptiness alone but to make room for something, and that something is the text of Scripture. Thus the prescribed prayers are the Psalms, the silences are silences around biblical readings, and even the mantras are Scriptural slogans, as the famous "Jesus prayer" of Byzantine monasticism. It is as we meditate on Scripture that Scripture can say to us what God intends it to say. If we do not meditate, or in our meditation imitate the Buddhists or Suffis or whomever, then Scripture will not speak to us.

The Scriptures live and have their churchly meaning within the church's *catechesis*. When the American church used to catechize its neophytes, this instruction had two purposes above all: providing Christians the access to Scripture without which they cannot function, and stocking their minds with Scripture's stories and phrases, so that they should be able to *think* like Christians. Precisely as our minds are *molded* by Scripture, Scripture says to us what God intends Scripture to say: the molding is here itself the message. And here something harsh must be said. It would be sad if the effect of these essays were to lay all the blame for the alienation on the academy. For the single most important cause of Scripture's alienation is that in the last twenty years the clergy of the American church stopped catechizing the neophytes of their congregations.

The Scriptures live and have their churchly meaning within the church's *homiletical* practice. When sermons were preached, they had texts — and it was best when those texts were not chosen by the preacher. Real sermons do not expound an idea or theme chosen by some individual, nor do they tell any story other than the story in or around the text. Rather, homilies and sermons and instructions communicate the gospel exactly as the speakers try to *say the same thing* that a scriptural text or texts say. As Scripture directly controls our homiletical discourse, it says what God wants it to say.

And now let me choose a few major issues of biblical hermeneutics and show how they are resolved not by theory but by the life of the church. I will, by necessity, discuss rather straightforward questions that inadequately represent the subtle and multifarious ways in which Scripture is actually interpreted in and by its churchly life.

Case one. From the first moment when churches arose that were predominantly gentile, it has been a question: Are the stories and commands and prayers and wisdom of Israel's Bible, our Old Testament, constitutive for the faith of the church today, or do they merely present the religious and historical background from which the church's faith springs? Or stated another way, Is the church's essential message wholly present in the New Testament so that the New Testament can in principle, if not in practice, *replace* the Old Testament and so that the permanent place of the Old Testament is only to help understand the New Testament? This is *the* fundamental question about the interpretation of the Old Testament, and when it has not been debated overtly it has been contested covertly.

The decision, I suggest, is not primarily made in learned debate. It is made in liturgical and homiletical practice. Here as elsewhere, let me instance my own ecclesial tradition. Our official rubrics now specify three readings for each main service: one from the Old Testament, one from the New Testament Epistles, and one from the Gospels. For centuries, however, our rubrics mandated no reading from the Old Testament, and many congregations, when they feel they must shorten the service, revert to that practice. Moreover, even when the Old Testament *is* read, in most congregations it never functions as the homiletical text.

But this of course, all by itself, decides the great question. For if the *Scripture* has been read when the Old Testament has not been read, or if although the Old Testament is read it never appears as the Scripture whose authority is to be honored, then the New Testament is made to be in principle the whole Scripture. And this then determines the *way* we read the Old Testament (if we do): We seek in it nothing but *antecedents* of the gospel's truth; it has nothing to say that is strictly its own. Thus *what* the Old Testament can say to us is mostly determined simply by *whether* it appears unavoidably and freely in the church's liturgy, by the liturgical role assigned to it.

Case two, of a very different sort. When I was a student at Heidelberg, the great scholars of the theological faculty there took turns preaching in the university church. It was in its fashion splendid. But every sermon began more or less the same way. After rereading the text, the eminent scholar would say, sometimes using the very same words as his predecessor, *"Nun aber, was sollen wir heute mit dieser altertümlichen Geschichte doch noch anfangen können?"* "Now — whatever are we to make of this uncanny ancient story, from a world so different from ours?"

It was presumed, you see, that we do *not* live in the biblical world, that its features and habits are strange to us — and, in fact, with the congregation there gathered, the presumption was no doubt correct. On that presumption, the Bible first had to be explained as an alien artifact from another world — which was always brilliantly done — and then enormous ingenuity expended to bridge the gap between the text so explained and our contemporary apprehensions — which did *not* always succeed so well. But what if those of us sitting there had already been familiar with the biblical world? What if the liturgy of German Protestantism enacted Scripture more richly? What if we had been properly catechized? How then could the exegete have proceeded? Again, what Scripture can say is determined by the character of the churchly life within which it is read.

Last case, of still a different sort. We here all agree, I suppose, that the Bible is somehow *authoritative*. But how does that work? For actual congregations of believers, I suggest, the matter is decided entirely by practice and very simply. When we hear preaching in the broadest sense, that is to say, when the church's servants call us verbally to faith and obedience, do we observe the speaker struggling to say what the Bible says? On more formal occasions, do we observe the preacher or teacher struggling somehow to say what a specific text says? If we do, we then and there *experience* the authority of Scripture. It is not a question of the preacher's or teacher's *success* in saying what Scripture says; the observable *effort* is by itself the necessary hermeneutical principle.

In many of our churches we have been experiencing denominational, diocesan, or synodical decisions and statements on moral, disciplinary, and even doctrinal matters, in which the plain teaching of Scripture is contravened. Let me provide an example. My own denomination recently issued a draft statement about sexuality that flatly contradicted what reasonable folk used to think Scripture plainly says about a variety of matters. Now the drafting committee had asked seminary-certified exegetes to tell them what guidance Scripture might give them. And the exegetes had said what such exegetes now always say when thus summoned: "You will just have to decide on your own." They were unable to offer anything definite.

Those experts were not being dishonest. They were simply reading Scripture as it will inevitably be read if the *classroom* is the only place it is read closely and seriously. In the homiletical practice of worshipping and teaching assemblies, on the other hand, reading Scripture closely and seriously means struggle, because lives and behavior are at stake and folk are not going to let us off with evasions. If *preaching* and *teaching* are seriously and determinedly scriptural in our churches, we *have* to struggle to say what Scripture says, and by the act itself necessarily cling to the conviction that Scripture does say *something*. The struggle itself is the hermeneutical principle. It is the parish clergy, not the academics, whose labor to read the text closely, and assumption of the struggle that means in the parish, will maintain the authority of Scripture, and whose failure to read the text closely will undercut the authority of Scripture.

III

Only now do I come to what was probably thought of as my whole assignment. Of course we do need explicit and systematic theory of biblical interpretation for those points in the church's life where liturgical, devotional, and catechetical imperatives are not directly the hermeneutical principle. Among the things the living church also does is *think*, and indeed chiefly about how to understand Scripture. So preachers and teachers have to *prepare* those addresses, and that means think about *how* to struggle to say what the text says. Liturgical commissions and local worship committees have to plan the rite and write the prayers, and that means thinking about *how* liturgy enacts the gospel. And we must think of these labors in today's situation, where preachers and commissions and theologians are indeed paralyzed by the gulf between the academic exegesis we have learned and the needs of the church.

I need not begin from scratch. For as it happens, the first explicit churchly theory of biblical exegesis was occasioned by a problem very like ours. The great Irenaeus, the second-century bishop of Lyon, lamented a captivity of Scripture to a pretentiously scholarly mode of interpretation alien to the purposes of the church, and countered with the first explicit reflection about proper churchly exegesis — the first, at least, of which we have a preserved document.

Gnostic teachers had devastated whole congregations of Irenaeus's diocese, attracting the faithful precisely by the seeming expertise of their biblical exegesis. According to Irenaeus, the procedure of these heretics was to treat Scripture as a sort of mine from which to dig spiritual wisdom. Their exegesis supposed that Scripture is a congeries of sayings and stories and commands and so forth, and that each component bit is a lump of ore from which we may extract precious insight if only we know the technique.

The gnostics' preferred extraction technique was allegory in the Hellenistic style, which looked for timeless truth over and above temporal narrative. Thus, as an example of an allegory that Irenaeus evidently found particularly irritating, from the circumstance in the Gospels that Jesus was silent for thirty years before beginning his preaching, we are to learn that within the eternal silence of the divine fullness there are precisely thirty great aeons.

But it was not so much the heretics' particular technology of wisdom extraction that Irenaeus denounced. He found the cause of their false teaching rather in two more general features of the gnostics' approach.

The first error of gnostic exegesis was to regard Scripture as a set of discrete opportunities to acquire or display spiritual and theological truth. The gnostics treated Scripture exactly as a great many preachers and catechists and teachers now treat it. They took Scripture's stories and sayings and laws one at a time, to be individually exploited by the discovery of whatever "idea" or "theme" or "story" it inspired.

The second error was the idea that the theological meaning of a text is something other than what it says. The gnostics assumed that the theological meaning of a scriptural story or saying or law must lie at some level other than the narrative or exhortatory or legal statement made by the language itself in its own context. It should be noted that rejecting this policy does not mean rejecting the church's traditional "spiritual" exegesis, for this exegesis was aimed precisely at discovering what a given passage in fact says in its total context of Scripture.

To contravene this sort of exegesis, Irenaeus laid down a

short list of hermeneutical rules. I heartily commend those very same rules to ourselves.

Rule one. Scripture is a whole. None of its constituent documents or traditions or pericopes or redactions is to be read in isolation from any other. The preacher preparing his or her sermon is not to stare at the given text, hoping for it to emit a bright idea or two. He or she is to read the text with a mind that brings with it the whole Bible, and labors to locate the text in that whole. Or, as Brevard Childs would say, the canonically shaped Bible is the unitary object of interpretation.

Rule two. Scripture *is* a whole because and only because it is one long *narrative*. All Scripture's detours and extensions and varieties of literary genre are to be read as moves within the telling of a single story. Therefore, for example, the single most important task of the preacher working on a parable-text is to ask what it means that *Jesus* told this parable, and that the one who told *this* parable is the risen Lord of all, and that it was *Israel* who heard and believed or did not believe, and that it is the *church* that retells it. When the preacher has worked out what place Jesus' telling of this precise parable has in Jesus' story as the climax of Israel's story, and what precise place the church's retelling of the parable has in Jesus' story with the church, the preacher *has* his or her sermon. All the rest of the preparation is mechanics and decoration.

Rule three. To be able to *follow* the single story and grasp Scripture whole, we need to know the story's general plot and *dramatis personae,* much as playgoers sitting down to a long, complex, and mystery-laden play need the playbill with its list of characters and synopsis of the plot. Scripture is *not* in *that* sense self-explanatory, that anyone simply coming across the unfamiliar book and reading through it is likely to find in it what God intends to be found. And it is not because Scripture is obscure that we need this prior knowledge, but rather precisely because Scripture is very clear about the kind of book it is.

Rule four. It is the *church* that knows the plot and *dramatis personae* of the scriptural narrative, since the church is one continuous community with the story's actors and narrators, as with its tradents, authors, and assemblers. The gnostics thought they needed special channels of information and access back to the revelation hidden in Scripture. And Irenaeus said they were right: they *did* need special channels to Scripture's truth, since they belonged to a community other than that in which Scripture appears and is at home. But the *church* needs no such channels to make contact with Scripture; it does not need to make contact with Scripture at all, since Moses and Isaiah and Paul and John and Irenaeus and you and I are all members of a single community.

Rule five. The church's antecedent knowledge of Scripture's plot and *dramatis personae*, without which she could not read the Bible as a whole, is contained in what Irenaeus calls "the rule of faith," the canon that the church propounds and teaches to her members regarding how to think and talk as Christians. When Irenaeus stated this rule, it came out as something much on the lines of the Apostles' Creed.

The church had been working on her "rule of faith" before Irenaeus and has been working on it ever since. By now, we even have a fairly short list of dogmas, and a few other bits and pieces of gospel truth, worked into pretty decent conceptual shape. If Irenaeus was right, there can be no churchly exegesis of the Bible that abstracts from this, that does not take the church's dogmas and ordinary teachings as playbill for the biblical drama.

Rarely do we appreciate the rather drastic point here. There can be no churchly reading of Scripture that is not activated and guided by the church's teaching. But to go back to an earlier point, there can be no reading of the Bible that is not churchly. Therefore there can be no reading of the unitary Bible that is not motivated and guided by the church's teaching. We will either read the Bible under the guidance of the church's established doctrine, or we will not read the Bible at all. When we attempt dogmatically rebellious or ignorant reading of Scripture, we will find only *dissecta membra* in our hands.

IV

Irenaeus assumes, rather than states, two points integral to his argument. He could assume them; we have to make them explicit.

The *unity* of the story told by the Bible is constituted by its having a single hero throughout: the God of Israel. There is only one biblical narrative for which the church assembled this book in the first place, to be in its entirety and all its parts witness to Jesus' resurrection and so to the action of a particular God. Apart from the Lord's self-identity as leading *dramatis persona* from creation to eschaton, the religious, conceptual, and cultural multiplicity of the genres and traditions and periods documented in Scripture is far too great for this collection to tell one story.

There is an exegetical mandate here. When we attempt to read the Bible, its unity will be available to us only as we attend to the self-identity of the biblical God. Therefore, among the questions with which we approach any text or set of texts or tradition or redaction — and the questions we will bring are of course unpredictably many and various — there is one that must always be asked: What does this piece of the Bible tell about the identity of God? *Which* God is it that Israel and the church worship?

Irenaeus's second assumption is that we do indeed know which God it is of whom Scripture speaks, because the "rule of faith" tells us: He is the specifically *Triune* God. Irenaeus's assumption is necessary: If we start out not knowing the identity of the God who is the agent of the biblical story, we cannot ask any particular text or part of the Bible what it says about that identity.

There is an exegetical mandate here also, and a very far-reaching one. To read the Bible whole, that is to read it as Bible, demands that the questions we bring to any text or set of texts or tradition or redaction — manifold and changeable as these questions will be — must be trinitarian questions. And to read the Bible whole, we must presume in advance that the doctrine of the Trinity is true, and that it must therefore also *answer* questions the Scripture raises for us.

V

This section abandons abstraction and illustrates how such neo-Irenaean exegesis works. I have chosen a particular body of Scripture as my case study because it is one I have been thinking about in several other connections.

Congregations are often puzzled or even offended by the texts of the Psalms they are assigned to pray. I suspect most of us deal with that by tuning the texts out altogether. But suppose we do not, or someone does not and asks one of us for explanation.

To refresh my experience of the problem, I let my desk Bible fall open to the Psalms. The first verses my eye lit upon were these: "O Lord my God . . . , if there is wrong in my hands . . . , then let the enemy . . . trample my life to the ground. . . . Judge me, O Lord, according to my righteousness. . ." (Psalm 7). I turned back a page, and read: "Make [my enemies] bear their guilt, O God. . ." (Psalm 5). Who can feel comfortable saying such things to God? He might do what we ask!

And then, of course, there are the many psalms where it is apparent that someone other than us is speaking, as on the next previous one: "I will tell of the decree of the Lord: He said to me, 'You are my son, today I have begotten you. Ask of me, and I will make the nations your heritage. . .'" (Psalm 2). The more dogmatically sophisticated will perhaps have been taught to think of Christ as the speaker here, and the more historically-critically sophisticated to think of some king in Jerusalem at his enthronement; either way, what are *we* doing praying these words — as many of us do at the feast of Transfiguration?

For guidance through this matter, let me turn to a central and famous instance within Scripture itself where a psalm is spoken by one other than the "historical" speaker: "My God, my God, why have you forsaken me?" It is, of course, the dying man Jesus who thus appropriates a lament of his ancestors. But the church's dogma teaches that the personhood of Jesus is identical with the personhood of God the Son. Precisely as a prayer of the man Jesus to his God, this psalm is here a word of God the Son to God the Father, a part of the interchange that constitutes the eternal inner life of God — and that mysterious fact, by the exegetical way, is the matter with which a preacher or teacher of this part of the passion-narrative must reckon.

But if it was God the Son speaking at the crucifixion, who was speaking on the occasions for which this prayer was originally conceived? How shall we identify the speaker of this prayer as it appears in the text of the Old Testament? The fathers of the church taught that the reality of the Son who is the Word transcends temporal separation and that therefore also in old Israel the final identity of the speaker must be God the Son, speaking in the midst of his Israelites. Indeed, that the second trinitarian Person is the Word that speaks also in canonical Israel and its Scriptures may be taken as the single great hermeneutical principle of the fathers after Irenaeus.

And then this psalm is assigned as *our* prayer, every Good Friday. How does *that* work? Let me recur to the fathers again. Reading the New Testament, they gathered much of its discourse in the figure of the *totus Christus*, "the total Christ," meaning the risen Christ *including and included in* his community. When Christ speaks, he does not speak as himself, but as identified with us. When we, his church, speak, we do not speak on our own, but as identified with him. And so when the dying Jesus cries out to his Father, this *is* our cry to his Father as our Father, in a dereliction we share with him. This is how we may and must pray this psalm.

But the psalm, precisely as a piece of inner-triune dialogue, was canonical Israel's cry as well. Irenaeus's principle that all Scripture tells one story has often been taken to mean that within the story the church *supersedes* — *replaces* — Israel.

101

Our century has been given urgent cause to rethink that theology. So here is a nice case where we have a strictly theological, even dogmatic decision to make before we can interpret a text. If we decide, as I think we must, that the church does *not* supersede Israel, then Israel according to the flesh, as Paul put it, and the church are *one* body of the *totus Christus*. So then, finally, "My God, my God, why have you forsaken me?" is a cry within the life of God, whose speaker is Christ with and as his one community of Abraham and Israelite kings and martyred prophets and Christian apostles and saints and you and me; and *that* is how we may and must pray it.

Now let us generalize for the whole Psalter whatever insight we have gotten from this analysis of one psalm. The speaker of the psalms is the *totus Christus*, the community of God's people from Abraham through the last Christian saint, as this community is one with the crucified and risen One. The *totus Christus* is indeed righteous with the divine righteousness of God the Son, and may and must indeed plead that righteousness before God the Father. The *totus Christus*, as Christ identified with us, is "the chief of sinners," and speaks to God also in this role. The *totus Christus* is indeed persecuted; he is Christ on the cross, and may and must indeed plead for victory over enemies. The *totus Christus* is the one individual Jesus, who spoke all those psalms that are in the first person singular. And he is the whole community of Israel and the church, who spoke all those psalms that are communal liturgy. And when we pray Israel's psalms as our own, we are *not* imposing a "Christian" meaning on texts that in themselves mean something else; we are praying them in the Triune space in which they were always prayed.

VI

And now we do finally have to deal with the great modern mode of exegesis taught in seminaries and university faculties — historical-critical exegesis. It is sometimes said that we are now in postmodern times and that therefore we may simply leave modernity's exegesis behind, together with the problems it caused. This will not, in my judgment, suffice, anymore than it sufficed when modernists simply left exegesis in the patristic style behind. I have made few direct references to the patron figure of our conference, Brevard Childs, but precisely at this point his contribution must be explicitly acknowledged. The way past the problem posed by historical-critical exegesis is not by relegating it to the past.

The *techniques* of historical-critical reading are not the essence of the matter. What constitutes modernity's upsetting relation to old texts is not techniques but a policy: that of maintaining critical awareness of *historical difference*. There is, for example, a vast span of history between Julius Caesar and Bill Clinton. Premodern societies experience such time separation as exactly what binds persons and events together in a common world, so that Clinton might well read the Gallic Wars for help with his current problems, on the assumption that both he and Caesar are in the business of politics. Modernity's "historical consciousness," *per contra*, experiences that time as a *separation*, so that Clinton and Caesar are each in their own historical world and the possibility of Caesar advising Clinton is problematic.

Historical consciousness, which is the dynamic at the heart of historical-critical reading, *keeps historical distance open*. Historical-critical reading maintains awareness of the distance between Caesar and Clinton or between Moses and what the Deuteronomists made of Moses or between the historical Jesus and us. Why should that have been an affliction for the faith? I suggest: because of a simple but profound mistake. It has been supposed that in the case of Scripture the historical distance kept open is between the story Scripture tells and us, or to put it another way, between the community of Israel and the primal church on the one hand and us on the other. On this supposition we of course must have the same problem relating to Scripture as Clinton has relating to Caesar.

But this is a boner, for we, in our time now, are merely

living the latest part of the very story Scripture tells; alternatively, the community from which Scripture comes and which is its immediate community of interpretation is simply the same community, the church, that we are. *Between* us and Scripture there simply is no historical distance to be kept open.

The historical distance that historical-critical reading of Scripture actually can and must keep open is the historical distance *within* Scripture's narrative; alternatively, it is the historical *compass* of the one community of Israel and the church. The historical distance that faith must indeed keep open, and of which historical-critical reading can maintain awareness, is the distance between Moses and the later prophets, between Jesus and Paul, between Paul and us, but never between the story as a whole and us, never between the biblical community as a whole and us. As Irenaeus said, we need no special exertions to join the community of which Scripture speaks or to profit from its story, because the community in question is the very one that we, as baptized, already belong to.

Historical-critical reading of Scripture has been an affliction for the faith because people have left the *church* out of their self-understanding as they have practiced it. Some of the pioneers of historical reading did this because they hated the church; many more because German Lutherans (who have been the great practitioners) *always* tend to leave the church out of their calculations.

Faith needs to maintain the historical distances within the biblical narrative, as these constitute the compass of the biblical community, because the story Scripture tells is not a myth. The function of the great myths is to tell what happens always and everywhere. Therefore, the narrative succession of the events they tell is unessential, and the myths always tend to collapse into abstract doctrines. It is possible to misread Scripture as myth: in current terms, as the metaphor or symbol of something or other. Again, parading the sin of my own denomination, it is possible to collapse the story Scripture tells into an illustration of the abstract doctrine that God loves sinners. But Scripture, for good or ill, does not present itself as myth. Under

104

the conditions of modernity, it is historical-critical reading that can keep us from mistaking this.

VII

Readers will have noticed that at nearly every step, the positions I advocated demand reckoning with the *church*. That is no accident. In my judgment, reclaiming the Bible for the church is in very large part accomplished by remembering that there *is* the church for which to claim the Bible.

And I hope readers will have noticed something else. I have not tried to load the blame for the Bible's alienation from the church on secular scholars but on the clergy and other churchly scholars like myself. Nobody else lost the Bible but we, and nobody else can reclaim it.

The Church, the Bible, and Dogmatic Theology

THOMAS HOPKO

A number of contemporary theologians have attempted to explain the relationship between the church and the Bible in the Orthodox tradition. The best single volume on the subject in my opinion is Father Georges Florovsky's collection of essays entitled *Bible, Church, Tradition: An Eastern Orthodox View*. This little book, together with Vladimir Lossky's classic article "Tradition and Traditions," published in *In the Image and Likeness of God*, provides, in my view, a thorough introduction to the subject. A number of books are now also available in English that can serve as "case studies" in showing the relationship between the church and the Bible in Eastern Orthodoxy. These works also demonstrate how this relationship works in practice, particularly in theological articulation and liturgical worship. (See appended bibliography.)

In this present essay I try to summarize the Orthodox view of the church and the Bible, and add some thoughts on the relationship between biblical exegesis and dogmatic theology in the Orthodox tradition.

The Church Community

For Eastern Orthodox Christians the church is the locus of God's full, perfect, and definitive self-revelation in history, the locus of God's most complete and compelling interaction with human beings. God did not give the world a book or a collection of writings. God rather called a community of people to which he is unconditionally devoted and in which he continually acts through his divine Word and Spirit.

God was constrained to constitute a community of elected people because of sin. Human beings are made to know God naturally. Sin destroys this natural knowledge. So God constitutes a people capable of cooperating with divine grace in and through which he makes himself known to those who are called, chosen, and faithful.

God's activity in his chosen community is an act of revelation, renewal, and redemption. The church is God's restoration of humanity in which the community itself is experienced as the "recreation of creation" (Gregory of Nyssa). The church is the community of people whose life is the holy communion in freedom, in spirit, and in truth, intended by God for human beings from the beginning. The church, therefore, is not an organization that God institutes because he wishes to impart supernatural truths by special divine revelations through especially established authorities to those who have faith so that he might add to the natural truths that all men and women can know by reason alone.

God's divinely called and constituted community identifies itself in history from the time of Abraham and his children until the present day. It maintains itself as a visible historical community by God's action in and with his human coworkers until now. Orthodox Christians claim that they can identify this community in every age and generation, knowing where it is, as well as where, at least fully and completely, it is not. Orthodox Christians believe that this community will continue to exist by God's grace until the end of the world.

Christ the Fulfillment

God's definitive act in the history of his covenanted people is the appearance of Jesus of Nazareth, whom the *qa'hal Israel*, to remain faithful to its calling, confesses to be God's Son and Word, the promised messiah, the fulfillment of all God's actions in history both within and beyond the bounds of the chosen community. The crucial ecclesial claim about Jesus is that while being a man with exactly the same humanity which all men and women share, he is also divine with the same divinity as God whom he knows from eternity as *Abba*, "Father."

God's people confess and worship Jesus the Messiah as God's uncreated Word incarnate as a real human being, born of Mary without human seed in order to die the shameful death of crucifixion in the form of a slave and to be raised from the dead and glorified forever in divine power "at the Father's right hand." The conviction that God has raised his Son Jesus from the dead and has made him Lord and Christ, the head over all things for the sake of "the church which is his body, the fullness of him who fills all in all" (Eph. 1:23), the "church of the living God, the pillar and bulwark of the truth" (1 Tim. 3:15), is the foundational conviction of Orthodox Christians.

This fundamental Orthodox Christian conviction is rooted in the experience of God in Christ in the community of people called by his name and empowered by his Spirit. The Holy Spirit, who is God's own Spirit and the Spirit of Christ, inspires all aspects of the community's life, which testify to its *synergeia* with God. The church is maintained in its being and life by the Spirit of Truth who brings to remembrance all that Jesus has said and done, and guides Christ's "members" into all truth by grace working through faith.

Church Life as Tradition

Every generation from Abraham's to our own has been marked by the foolishness and faithlessness of most of God's chosen

109

people that have led to heresies and schisms in and from the community. In dealing with the inevitable divisions that arise within and from the church, those who are genuinely faithful to God become recognized and approved (see 1 Cor. 11:18). For in every age and generation only certain of God's people preserve the integrity of the church's life and teaching, handing it over and handing it down to others who are faithful. The essential duty of a church member, in the Orthodox perspective, indeed his and her *only* task, is to be numbered among the "genuine" within God's believing and worshiping ecclesial community.

The life of God's covenanted community that is handed down and handed over from Abraham's time until today transcends all of the witnesses and testimonies to it. The church's life is something more, indeed even something radically *other*, than anything that can be said about it. Irreducible to any and all of its external expressions and forms, the community's life that is empowered and maintained in the faithful by God's Holy Spirit is known by the Orthodox as "Holy Tradition."

As the church lives through history, its life, which is also its communal "memory," is expressed in stories, rites, rules, teachings, and traditions that are told, recorded, read, and interpreted — and retold, rerecorded, reread, and reinterpreted — in the light of its ongoing interaction with God and with the world in which the community lives and to which it is organically connected and related. The retelling, recording, interpreting, and reinterpreting of God's interaction with his people becomes in this way itself an essential element of the community's ongoing life, its Holy Tradition. Indeed, this traditional activity is the church's life itself.

Testimonies to Tradition

The problem inevitably arises in the church community about the determination and selection of the memories, stories, rituals, and teachings that have emerged in both written and unwritten forms that faithfully witness to God's action with his people and the people's life with God — with a corresponding rejection of that which is spurious, undependable, and untrue. And the problem also presents itself about how the testimonies that the church community unanimously seals and approves are to be interpreted, understood, and applied in its ongoing life, both for itself and in relationship to those outside the covenant.

The accepted testimonies to authentic church life, to Holy Tradition, include first and foremost the writings produced in, by, and for the community of faith that witness to God's action in the people and the people's relationship with God; and so to the church's history, experience, worship, and teaching. We now simply call these writings the Bible.

The community's testimonies to Tradition also include the church's formal expressions of worship, the universally received liturgical and sacramental rites in which the church actualizes itself as God's People, the body and bride of Christ. The church's liturgical worship and sacramental ritual are themselves substantially biblical in content, spirit, and form.

The testimonies to the Church's Tradition also include the doctrinal definitions that the church universally accepts in its creedal symbols; the canons for community organization and behavior; the glorified men and women, that is, the canonized "saints" whose lives and teachings are formally presented in the community for imitation and emulation; and finally they include the church's art and architecture, especially the iconographic testimony by which the people confess their faith and express their theological convictions in the context of liturgical worship.

While all of the testimonies to the church's life, history, and teaching are subordinated to the life of the church herself, that is, to Holy Tradition, and while all of these testimonies are organically interrelated and mutually enabling and enlightening, the church's canonized writings that we now call the Bible have a unique and special importance and significance. This is particularly true of the canonized writings of the apostolic Christian community that testify to Jesus as Israel's Messiah, God's Son and Word: the Creator, Savior, Head, and Lord of all things.

For Orthodox Christians, the writings that the church community canonizes as its accepted testimony to Jesus, particularly the four Gospels, have a unique authority in the church. In their interpretation of the Hebrew Scriptures in relation to Jesus they virtually *determine* the church's life and self-understanding and, so, its liturgical worship, theological doctrine, ethical norms, and spiritual activity in all of its manifold aspects. The risen Christ, present in the community as the Holy Spirit in word and sacrament, opens the minds of believers to the understanding of the Scriptures (cf. Luke 24:27, 44).

The Task of Theology

Much has been said and written in the Orthodox Church in this century, especially its second half, about the nature and task of theology. Severe criticisms have been leveled against the "Western captivity" of teaching and piety in the Orthodox Church, particularly since the seventeenth century. Many contemporary Orthodox scholars and theologians have noted the discrepancy between the church's Holy Tradition testified to in the Bible and in her liturgical and sacramental services and in the lives and teachings of her saints, and the material contained in seminary textbooks and systematic theologies as well as in popular catechisms and devotional manuals. These critical thinkers have called for the recovery of a vibrant biblical, liturgical, ascetical, and mystical theology inspired and informed by the church's actual life, that is, her Holy Tradition. They have done this in different ways, with different emphases.

Some stress the need for a return to the church's liturgical worship, the *lex orandi,* as a living source of theological discourse and articulation. Others call for a "creative return to the fathers." Still others focus on ascetical and mystical life, with theology defined as the "climax of purity," with the verbal witness to the church's faith and life seen as the product of ceaseless prayer and constant spiritual striving. All who call for such renewal, however, whatever their particular emphasis, underscore the necessity of holding together all of the testimonies to the church's life — Scripture, liturgy, conciliar decrees, canons, icons, patristic writings, lives of saints — in vital harmony and coinherence. And all emphasize the foundational authority of the Bible, especially the New Testament writings, and most especially the four Gospels.

With an understanding of Tradition as the church's life and memory that transcends in silence all of the community's external expressions and forms, there can never be a full and final expression of the church's teachings in a work of dogmatic theology. There can also never be a complete "systematic theology." What can and must and inevitably always will be are attempts to determine what is genuinely "of the church" on a given question, and on any number of given issues. This will be done by discovering and demonstrating a unanimous and harmonious witness on the matters in question from all of the church's testimonies to its life and experience, beginning first of all with the biblical testimony.

The Task of Dogmatic Theology

For the Orthodox, dogmatic theology is the attempt to identify and eventually to articulate and explain in a *synthetic*, rather than *systematic*, way the vision and experience that has been held always, everywhere, and by all who live the life of God's covenanted community headed by the risen Christ and guided by the Holy Spirit; that is, by all who are Orthodox. The task of discovering, explaining, and synthesizing the church's vision and experience will be continually reattempted and renewed because the church is a living organism existing in a constantly changing world.

New claims are constantly made about reality. New questions are raised and new challenges are presented to Christian faith and life from both within and outside the covenanted community. The task of dogmatic theology is therefore constantly present. New insights that are compatible with the "faith once for all delivered to the saints" must be affirmed and integrated into church life and teaching, while opinions contrary to divine truth must be exposed and rejected by the community of faith. In this perspective, no issue is irrelevant to dogmatic theology and no question is out of order. Just the opposite. Dogmatics by definition deals with all questions and issues. This is its task. Those with the charism of theological articulation take up the questions presented in and to the church in an attempt to discover what, if anything, the church *qua church* witnesses and teaches about them. They attempt to articulate and explain what they discover in their examination of the church's testimonies. They struggle to find the church's "mind," understood to be the "mind of Christ," and to describe and explain it as clearly as they can by the guidance of the Spirit.

Dogmatic theology, in this way, does not begin with any particular philosophy, nor does it depend on any specific philosophical presuppositions. It is not based on any philosophical vision or method coming from outside the church community. It often, though not always or necessarily, articulates the church's vision and experience in terms of a certain philosophical language or set of philosophical categories because of the specific time and place in which it is carried out, and in terms of the isses and questions with which it specifically deals. But the church's dogmatic theologians say what they do because they are living the church's life and are personally engaged with the living expressions of this life that constitute its fabric and enfleshment in history, that is, once again, the church's canonized Scriptures, liturgical and sacramental rites, conciliar definitions, creedal symbols, canonical norms, and canonized saints.

Dogmatic theology, in this perspective, is always *church* dogmatics. It is an articulation of the vision of unchanging divine truth formulated in and for the believing community, not for those outside who, without the ecclesial experience, cannot possibly understand it. In this sense dogmatic theology, and theology generally, differs radically from preaching, apologetics, and Christian "philosophy," understood as what Christians may try to convey about reality to those outside the church on the basis of what they have come to see from within, but which does not depend on ecclesial experience for its understanding.

With this understanding of dogmatics, Christian theologians must be capable of proving that their theological syntheses are adequate to the church's life and experience according to all of its witnesses. And so they must demonstrate that their doctrine is adequate to the Christ who is witnessed to in the Bible and known in the church's liturgical, sacramental, and mystical experience. And so, finally, they must produce an articulation of the faith that is, to use the traditional Orthodox word, *theoprepeis,* adequate, fitting, and proper to God himself.

Biblical Exegesis and Church Dogmatics

In this perspective there can be no church dogmatics without a proper interpretation of the Bible. Biblical exegesis is absolutely necessary for dogmatic theology. It also follows that the Bible can be interpreted only within the church in and for which it has been written, the church to whose life and teaching it bears witness, the church whose ongoing Holy Tradition provides the hermeneutical setting for its proper interpretation and application.

The covenanted community, and so especially the dogmatic theologian, welcomes everything that can illumine the Bible and help believers to understand the biblical writings and to apply the scriptural testimony more clearly, deeply, and adequately to human thinking and behavior. All historical, literary, philological, archaeological, and cultural studies that can assist in clarifying and explaining biblical texts are received with gratitude, including studies accomplished by those outside the ecclesial community that are sound and true, and therefore, from the church's perspective, are judged to be inspired by the same Holy Spirit who dwells in the church. For the Holy Spirit (who is neither a magician nor a mechanic) freely inspires all study that is accurate, interacting with the honest, good-willed scholar (whether she or he realizes it or not) in order to reveal the truth.

What is not welcomed or accepted in the Orthodox perspective, however, is the claim that the Bible can be properly understood by critical studies alone (studies that themselves arrive at greatly differing conclusions), or that critical studies can in and by themselves be technically and properly called *theology*, or even *exegesis* (though some may use this word, inaccurately perhaps, from an Orthodox perspective, for the results of their scientific work). To remove the Bible from its organic churchly setting and to attempt to "exegete" it outside its ecclesial context is itself "uncritical" and "unscientific," since such a method of reading and interpreting the Scriptures is contrary to the testimony of the writings themselves, as well as to the testimony of the church that produced them.

In this perspective, therefore, it is necessary not only to make the effort of "reclaiming the Bible for the church" so that dogmatic theology can be properly biblical and churchly; it is also necessary to undertake the task of reclaiming, perhaps even *rediscovering*, the church as a concrete, historical, visible community, for the sake of the Bible, so that there can be proper biblical exegesis and dogmatic theolgy. For without the historical church with a living Holy Tradition that transcends all of its formal and external expressions and testimonies, including those of the community's canonized Scriptures, there is little hope for the Bible to be anything other than a collection of writings that anyone can interpret, by whatever methods, for whatever reasons, to whatever ends. And without the church there can also be no dogmatic theology, and indeed, no *theologia* in the traditional sense of the word at all. There can only be a variety of quasi-Christian "worldviews," more or less churchly and more or less biblical, idiosyncratically produced and presented by brilliant minds in ever new and original ways for those who, for whatever reasons, are interested in such things.

In the Orthodox experience there can finally be no reclaiming of the Bible for the church without a more fundamental and original reclaiming of the church and its living Tradition for the sake of the Bible.

Bibliography

Barrois, Georges A. *The Face of Christ in the Old Testament.* Crestwood, N.Y.: St. Vladimir's Seminary Press, 1974.

———. *Scripture Readings in Orthodox Worship.* Crestwood, N.Y.: St. Vladimir's Seminary Press, 1977.

Breck, John. *The Power of the Word in the Worshiping Church.* Crestwood, N.Y.: St. Vladimir's Seminary Press, 1986.

———. *Spirit of Truth — I. The Origins of Johannine Pneumatology.* Crestwood, N.Y.: St. Vladimir's Seminary Press, 1991.

———. "Orthodoxy and the Bible Today." In *The Legacy of St. Vladimir,* 141-157. Crestwood, N.Y.: St. Vladimir's Seminary Press, 1990.

Englezakis, Benedict. *New and Old in God's Revelation. Studies in Relations between Spirit and Tradition in the Bible.* Crestwood, N.Y.: St. Vladimir's Seminary Press, 1982.

Florovsky, Georges. *Bible, Church, Tradition: An Eastern Orthodox View.* Belmont, Mass.: Nordland Publishing Company, 1972.

Hopko, Thomas. *The Orthodox Faith.* Vol. III, Bible and Church History, 1-115. New York: Department of Religious Education, Orthodox Church in America, 1979.

———. "The Bible in the Orthodox Church." In *All the Fulness of God,* 49-90. Crestwood, N.Y.: St. Vladimir's Seminary Press, 1982.

Kesich, Veselin. *The Gospel Image of Christ.* Rev. ed. Crestwood, N.Y.: St. Vladimir's Seminary Press, 1992.

————. *The First Day of the New Creation*. Crestwood, N.Y.: St. Vladimir's Seminary Press, 1982.

————. "Criticism, the Gospel and the Church," *St. Vladimir's Seminary Quarterly* 10 (1966): 134-62.

————. "Research and Prejudice," *St. Vladimir's Theological Quarterly* 14 (1970): 28-47.

————. "The Orthodox Church and Biblical Interpretation," *St. Vladimir's Theological Quarterly* 37 (1993): 343-51.

Lossky, Vladimir. "Tradition and Traditions." In *In the Image and Likeness of God*, 141-68. Crestwood, N.Y.: St. Vladimir's Seminary Press, 1974.

Schmemann, Alexander. "The Sacrament of the Word." In *The Eucharist*, 65-80. Crestwood, N.Y.: St. Vladimir's Seminary Press, 1987.

————. *Liturgy and Tradition. Theological Reflections of Alexander Schmemann*, edited by Thomas Fisch. Crestwood, N.Y.: St. Vladimir's Seminary Press, 1990.

Staniloae, Dumitru. "Revelation through Acts, Words and Images" and "Revelation as Gift and Promise." In *Theology and the Church*, 109-80. Crestwood, N.Y.: St. Vladimir's Seminary Press, 1980.

Tarazi, Paul Nadim. *Introduction to the Old Testament*. Vol. 1, Historical Traditions. Crestwood, N.Y.: St. Vladimir's Seminary Press, 1991.

————. *Introduction to the Old Testament*. Vol. 2, *Prophetic Traditions*. Crestwood, N.Y.: St. Vladimir's Seminary Press, 1994.

Zizioulas, John D. *Being As Communion. Studies in Personhood and the Church*. Crestwood, N.Y.: St. Vladimir's Seminary Press, 1985.

The Canon as the Voice
of the Living God

ELIZABETH ACHTEMEIER

In 1966, Karl Barth published a little book entitled *Homiletik*. The book was translated and published in English in 1991 (Louisville: W/JK Press), and in that book, Barth had a good deal to say about the use of Scripture in the church. I would like to quote a few of his sentences to you:

> The fact of the canon tells us simply that the church has regarded these scriptures as the place where we can expect to hear the voice of God. The proper attitude of preachers does not depend on whether they hold on to a doctrine of inspiration but on whether or not they expect God to speak to them here. (p. 78)

The Christian church is the community that expects to hear God speaking through its Scriptures. It is that community which has been formed and sustained by the God who addresses it through those events and words that are preserved for us in the Bible. And it is still the community that hears the divine voice uttered through its canon. As John Calvin has put it,

Enlightened by (the Holy Spirit), we no longer believe either on our own judgment or that of others, that the Scriptures are from God; but, in a way superior to human judgment, feel perfectly assured — as much so as if we beheld the divine image visibly impressed on it — that it came to us, by the instrumentality of men, from the very mouth of God. (*Institutes*, I.vii.5)

The Christian church lives and moves and has its being from the God who speaks through its canon by the Holy Spirit.

Because much of the church in this country no longer believes or expects to hear God speaking through its Scriptures, it therefore is not very Christian anymore. And, of course, the results in our mainline churches have been simply devastating.

Over the last decade, I have been involved through my speaking and writing in the debate that is going on in the church over three pressing issues — the issue of sexuality and homosexuality, the issue of feminism, and the issue of abortion. (See, for example, Terry Schlossberg and Elizabeth Achtemeier, *Not My Own: Abortion and the Marks of the Church* [Grand Rapids: Eerdmans, Spring 1995]). But the frustration that one experiences in trying to carry on that debate apart from any common recognition of a canon for the church is sometimes almost overwhelming. For example, what does the church have to say to a woman who claims, "My body is my own," if the church does not know from its canon that we are not our own, but bought with a price and adopted in our baptisms as God's sons and daughters? Or what can the church say to the feminist discussion about the nature of God if it does not hear from its canon that God is not identical with the vital forces of nature, but rather is holy God, totally other than all he has made? Or what can the church say about sexual morality, unless it knows itself from its Scripture to be a covenant people, redeemed from the law, and yet given commandments to guide it in its new life in Christ? The mainline churches are in chaos over these issues, but the debates will never be settled until the church once more confesses that it has a canon, through which there speaks to us the voice of the Triune God.

Certainly the whole enterprise of historical criticism is partly responsible for the chaos. Despite all that such science has taught us — despite the debt that we owe to the critics for opening up to us the language and history, the literature and geography, the sociology and archaeology pertaining to the Bible — it cannot be doubted that some critics have felt their science sufficient unto itself and therefore unneedful of any divine and transcendent Word beyond them.

And, of course, that human pride which has always claimed to be self-sufficient and which has affected the human race throughout its history is in our time the terrible disease of the mainline churches. The radical feminists among us — and I emphasize the word "radical," because we must always distinguish between feminism as fairness and radical feminism as ideology — have abandoned any thought of an authoritative canon and replaced it with reliance on their own subjective experiences, shared in their communities called Womenchurch. The Scriptures are, they say, simply ancient documents, born out of the customs and traditions of ancient patriarchal societies, and then assembled and interpreted solely by males. And so all of that patriarchalism and androcentrism is to be rejected by liberated twentieth-century females, they say, who find their goddess in all things and indeed in themselves and in their sexuality. Said a radical feminist on the Duke University campus some time ago, "Women do not need to be redeemed; they just need to be affirmed." But the real tragedy is that some American church leaders and clergy, who have lost their canon, have agreed with such nonsense.

It is not only the historical critics who are to blame, of course, but also those preachers in countless churches who, instead of preaching from the Scriptures, are preaching from the commentaries — who, instead of wrestling with the biblical texts when they are writing a sermon, have reached first for the *Interpreter's Bible* or Barclay or *The Layman's Bible Commentary* or *Proclamation*, and from those books thought to dis-

121

cern the Word of God for his church. To be sure, there are hundreds of faithful biblical preachers in this country. But there are also hundreds who would be astounded to think that God actually speaks through the Bible and who have never had that expectation. And so the sin of human pride continues: We think we can go it on our own.

Indeed, is it not finally that primeval sin that so infects our churches nowadays — the thought that our wisdom is all and that the Bible has nothing to say to us about the working of the Spirit, except what we ourselves bring to its text? Deconstructionism, we can call it — the theory that the Scriptures have no objective truth, but rather bear only the meaning that the interpreter brings to them. As a result, in my Presbyterian denomination at least, the theory is very widespread that every interpretation of Scripture is valid and is to be taken seriously, a view that ignores the benefits of historical criticism. And so the church is left to guide its course by the competing voices of dozens of caucuses, and the life of the church has become a power struggle among those competing groups.

Losing our canon, through which speaks the Holy Spirit, the voice of the sovereign God, we in the church have almost lost our church. And were it not for the promise of Christ that the gates of hell will never prevail against his little colony of heaven, we would indeed be crushed and despairing and destroyed (1 Cor. 4:8-9) by our present situation. But we know — all of us here know — that God continues to speak through his Word. As the great Lutheran preacher, Paul Scherer, once remarked, "God did not stop speaking when his book went to press." And so now our task is to reawaken the church to that divine voice by which it is addressed, to reclaim for the church the canon of the Scriptures through which God in his mercy reveals himself.

How should we go about that task? To tell you the truth, I know of no other way than to let the Scriptures prove themselves by always presenting them. No one believes that God speaks through his Word until they hear it. And no argument can convince the unbeliever apart from the work of the Spirit.

"Faith comes from what is heard," writes Paul, "and what is heard comes by the preaching of Christ" (Rom. 10:17, RSV). And it is the preaching of Christ — the testimony of faith that there is beyond our human words a transcendent Word — it is that alone which can awaken and renew the church. From the pulpit and in classrooms and in writings, in all our lives and doings, we scholars and teachers, we clergy and laity must convey our urgent message of the gospel. It is no longer sufficient in a classroom or book or pulpit to deal with strictly human matters. Always there must be the affirmation that God is involved and speaks. And perhaps then the church will begin to catch the sound of that transcendent voice addressing it.

But I have some firm convictions about so reclaiming the canon for the church, and all of them have to do with how we approach the Scriptures. First of all, I am quite convinced that the church will not reclaim its canon until it once again includes in that canon the books of the Old Testament. The church as a whole lost the Old Testament somewhere between 1875 and 1933, when developmentalism was the fashion. The Old Testament was, it came to be thought, simply the record of the natural evolutionary development of religious ideas and institutions, from their lowest form to their highest, beginning with the prophetic faith and proceeding to the New Testament, with the teachings of Jesus representing the highest peak of the development. And so there was born the History of Religions school. But most important, there came to the fore the belief that the Old Testament was an earlier primitive stage in the development of religion, which then could be discarded for the higher spiritual truths of the New Testament. Walter Eichrodt finally gave the lie to such developmentalism with his epic-making *Theologie des Alten Testaments* (ET *Theology of the Old Testament*; Louisville: Ky.: Westminster/John Knox, 1967), and that let loose the floodgate of biblical theology, which found its most prevalent form after the Second World War in the Biblical Theology movement (see B. Childs, *Biblical Theology in Crisis*; Louisville, Ky.: Westminster, 1970).

123

Yet, in a sense, the church has never recovered from developmentalism, and the average layperson in the pew and even many preachers still regard the Old Testament as an unnecessary prelude to the "real" New Testament Bible. But if we speak of reclaiming our roots in the Scriptures, we must not see those roots as located only in the New Testament. Despite the Old Testament lessons given in the three-year lectionary, there are still many clergy in this country who preach only from the New Testament. And of course the ignorance of the contents of the Old Testament, among both clergy and laity alike, is enough to make one shudder.

Perhaps it is therefore no surprise that a good number of contemporary theologians have divorced the figure of Jesus from his historical background in Israel. Separated from the history in the Old Testament, Jesus can be viewed as a mythic figure or ideal or metaphor, a trend in modern theology against which Carl Braaten has written so eloquently in his book *No Other Gospel* (Minneapolis: Augsburg/Fortress, 1992).

The truth of the matter is, of course, that Jesus Christ cannot be known except in relation to the Old Testament, for as Childs states in his *Biblical Theology*, "The most striking feature of the New Testament is that it bears its witness to the radically new (which is Jesus Christ) in terms of the old. The gospel of Jesus Christ is understood by means of a transformed Old Testament" (p. 93).

Who is Jesus Christ? The answer of the New Testament is that he is "the son of David, the son of Abraham" (Matt. 1:1), the one written about "in the law of Moses and the prophets and the psalms" (Luke 24:44). He gathers up all four of the major theological complexes of the Old Testament into himself — the theology of the hexateuch, of the monarchy, of the prophets, and of wisdom.

This is not to say that there is nothing new in the New Testament. Of course there is. Someone greater than Solomon is there, someone greater than the prophets, and David, and Moses. "Before Abraham was, I am," Jesus said. And so many prophets and righteous people longed to see what you see, and did not see it, and to hear what you hear, and did not hear it. And thus, you who are least in the kingdom of heaven are greater than even John the Baptist. But Jesus Christ is also identified in the New Testament as the fulfillment and final interpretation of the Old Testament.

For example, for those New Testament witnesses who employ the royal traditions, Jesus is variously the Messiah, the long-awaited Son of David, the shepherd-prince promised by Ezekiel (John 10), the High Priest after the order of Melchizedek (Hebrews), exalted to the right hand of the Father.

For those who tell the story of Jesus' earthly life and death, Jesus is diversely a new Moses (Matthew), the prophet like Moses who is to come (Acts), and the Suffering Servant who gives his life as a ransom for many (Mark). He is the one who frees Israel from her final slavery, who institutes the new covenant in his blood, who makes the perfect sacrifice for sin once for all. He is, in 1 Peter, the stone which the builders rejected, which becomes the head of the corner; in 1 Corinthians, the rock of stumbling for the Jews and foolishness for the Gentiles; in the Gospels, the ideal righteous man of the Psalms, suffering and praising his Father from the cross.

And for those New Testament witnesses who concentrate on the fullness of the incarnation, Jesus is, in various traditions, the new obedient son Israel, called out of Egypt and obedient in the wilderness, the incarnate temple and covenant and light and lamb in his role as the Servant in the Fourth Gospel. He is Isaiah's cornerstone of the new congregation of faith on Zion, the true vine, the true manna, the bread and drink of life, and even the incarnate promised land. In short, Jesus Christ is, in the New Testament, the Word of the Old made flesh — the new promised action of God (Isa. 43:19) that nevertheless gathers up the promises of the Old Testament and brings them to their final interpretation and conclusion, as Second Isaiah had said God would do.

There are Christian scholars in this country who steadfastly refuse to join the two Testaments and who ignore the fact of the canon by referring to the Old Testament as the

Hebrew scriptures. But in the radically new action of incarnating himself in his Son, God himself has joined the two Testaments, thereby enfleshing his eighteen hundred years of interaction with his people Israel. And unless that be known in the church, its Lord Jesus Christ also cannot be known.

Indeed, unless the Old Testament is known, the church cannot even know who it is, for we as the Body of Christ are also, in Paul's thought, the Israel of God (Gal. 6:16), the true circumcision (Phil. 3:3), the wild branches grafted into the root of Israel (Rom. 11:17-24). Or in Ephesians, we now are members of the commonwealth of Israel (2:12-18) and therefore, as in 1 Peter 2, the inheritors of the titles "chosen race, royal priesthood, a holy nation" (2:9; cf. Exod. 19:6). In short, we have become members of the new Israel in Jesus Christ, and we now are to understand ourselves at least partly in terms of that people of the old covenant. And so the church has to ask itself, Who was Israel, and on what basis was it constituted, and what was it to do? For in becoming the new Israel in Christ, we have become heirs to the promises of the Old Testament (cf. Gal. 4:7).

It was characteristic of the prophets of the Old Testament to promise not only that the new people of God would not only be radically new — the law written on their hearts (Jer. 31:33) and the humble spirit of faith and obedience their way (cf. Zeph. 3:12; Ezek. 36:27; Isa. 28:16). The prophets, and especially Second Isaiah, also promised that the life of the new people of God would recapitulate that of the old. And so it is that we find our life in the church prefigured in the life of Israel.

Consider the correspondences between Israel and the church. Both are redeemed out of slavery by the loving action of God, long before they have done one thing to deserve it. Israel is delivered from slavery in Egypt, we (the church) from the slavery of sin and death. And so Jesus speaks of his cross in Luke 9:31 as his "exodus," and the cross in the New Testament is seen as that redemptive act which is parallel to God's redemption of Israel out of Egypt. Both Israel and the church are adopted as the son or children of God — Israel at the time of the exodus, we at our baptisms. Both are brought to the table of covenant — Israel of old to Sinai and we to the Lord's Supper. Both of us at that table promise to walk by the covenant commandments. "All that the LORD has spoken we will do" (Exod. 19:8), Israel vows, while those of us who "do earnestly repent of our sins" and "intend to lead a new life, following the commandments of God," draw near with faith and take the holy sacrament.

As God's covenant people, both Israel and the church are set apart for God's purpose as his holy nation, and both are his kingdom of priests, with the responsibility of speaking the knowledge of him to the rest of the world. Both Israel and the church are set on a journey toward a promised place of rest, and both are God's visited people, who are accompanied on their pilgrimage by the presence of God himself.

The life of the new Israel in Christ, in many respects, recapitulates the life of the old, and there, writ large on the pages of the Old Testament, the church can see itself in its relation to God. And so the Old Testament becomes for the church its own story by which it knows who it is, by which it is warned, by which it is guided and sustained, and through which it can believe that God is faithful to his Word.

The Old Testament is our story, by virtue of God's act in Jesus Christ. Which means, to go further, that the Old Testament now speaks to us as Israel. It is not only in a scheme of promise and fulfillment that we now hear the Old Testament — a scheme that some have tried to impose on the entire lectionary. No, the Old Testament now speaks both its words of judgment and grace to us as it once spoke to Israel, because we too are now the Israel of God. The Old Testament now gives its own unique revelation. For example, when God declares through Amos, in chapter 3, "You only have I known of all the families of the earth; therefore I will punish you for all your iniquities" (v. 2), that is not only a Word to the Israel of the eighth century B.C. That is now also a Word spoken directly to the church, and the church must reckon with the judgment contained in that Word. Or when Israel's ingratitude is so manifest there in the wilderness in Num. 11:6 — "There is nothing at all but this manna to look at," she complains — the church must also see itself harboring the same ingratitude for God's many benefits. Out of such immediate address by the Scriptures — an immediacy long known to the most simple reader of the Bible, for whom we must always make room — biblical preaching and teaching are born. And while historical criticism can exercise a useful check by making us conscious of the distance between the biblical text and our own situation (so too Childs, *Biblical Theology*, p. 88), it finally must also be recognized that God speaks to us directly from the book of the old covenant.

Finally, let me say a word about the relationship of the two testaments in a scheme of *Heilsgeschichte*. And by *Heilsgeschichte* I mean a history into which the Word of God is spoken and which is then moved forward and shaped by the Word until the Word is fulfilled. Our people in the church suffer from the fact that they hear the Bible only in bits and pieces. They hear only one or two passages read on Sunday morning. They study only one book or portions of a book in Bible classes. They know a few of the familiar stories and they hear verses quoted from time to time — at Christmas ("Unto us a child is born") or perhaps at Easter ("He is risen"). But most of our people never learn how the whole canon hangs together. They do not know where the individual pieces fit into a continuous story, and they do not know the overarching theme of the whole canon. I sometimes therefore challenge preachers to present the whole story. "Could you," I ask them, "tell the story of the whole Bible, with God as the subject, in a twenty minute sermon?" For certainly the story needs to be told, if the Bible is to be reclaimed for the church. But how does one do it? How should we present the one story of the Scriptures?

In working with groups of laypeople, it has become my practice to tell the canon's story in terms of the four promises to Abraham, with the primeval history of Genesis 1 to 11 serving as the reason for the promises. And to those four promises of land, descendants, covenant, and blessing is then added the promise to David, in 2 Samuel 7, that there will never be lacking an heir to sit upon the Davidic throne.

The whole story of the Bible, then, concerns how God keeps those promises. Certainly the hexateuch sees three of them — of land, descendants, and covenant — fulfilled by the end of the book of Joshua, while the time in the land becomes a test of whether Israel will be a source of blessing to all the nations on earth. The promise to David is added during his reign in the tenth century B.C., but then in the time of the subsequent monarchy and prophets every one of the promises seems taken back in the holocaust of the Babylonian exile. The land is lost, Israel's population is drastically reduced, the covenant is broken, the Davidic king is prisoner in Babylonia, and Israel, says Jeremiah, has become a source of cursing and hissing rather than a blessing. Yet, even in the midst of the ruins, the prophets cling to God's Word, and promise that there will again be a return to the land, a new multiplication of population, a new Davidic king, and a new covenant, with Israel "the third with Egypt and Assyria, a blessing in the midst of the earth" (Isa. 19:24).

It is then when the "Son of David, the Son of Abraham" is born in the city of David, and when his life, death, and resurrection are accomplished by God, that Paul can write to the Corinthians, "All the promises of God find their Yes in him" (2 Cor. 1:20 RSV), for Jesus Christ becomes, according to the New Testament, the new David, the incarnate covenant and land, the cornerstone of a new people as many as the stars of the heaven, and the source of God's blessing for all the families of the earth. In Jesus Christ, God completes his work of redemption, so that Christ from the cross can cry, "It is finished!" The Word of the Old Testament does not return to God void, but accomplishes that which God purposes and prospers in the thing for which he sent it (Isa. 55:11).

To be sure, Jesus Christ, the fulfillment, then gives new promises from God, and the history continues into our present day: "Whoever lives and believes in me shall never die" (John

129

11:26); "Lo, I am with you always to the close of the age" (Matt. 28:20); "I will not leave you desolate; I will come to you" (John 14:18). But first of all Jesus Christ completes and fulfills and transforms that which God began in Israel, and in those terms, I believe, the whole canon holds together. "The Word of our God will stand forever." It stands forever because of Jesus Christ. In a sense, that is the theme of the canon. And by the mercy of God, it certainly still witnesses to our salvation, our hope, and the source of all our joy.

Scriptural Word and
Liturgical Worship

AIDAN J. KAVANAGH, O.S.B.

I take it as axiomatic in the Judaeo-Christian tradition that the scriptural Word of God and (for Christians) the incarnate Word of God are and have been worshipfully received. The axiom implies several things.

First, God's Word is never idle. It is spoken — a lively Word — to be heard and kept for the creation and salvation of all, for the life of the world. For this reason if for no other this Word is received by us with reverence, obedience, and thanksgiving — that is, worshipfully.

Second, the Word gets *written* within communities that regard the Word worshipfully. This means that rather than being Scripture's stepchild, worship is Scripture's home. Thus worship is not merely a function of Scripture; together, both Scripture and worship are a function of the Word spoken and received. Neither Scripture nor worship is *about* God; they are *of* God, each in its own proper way. They are strictly correlative; neither can exist without the other. To take a lead from Luther, if the authority of Scripture arises from its being the cradle in which Christ lies, then Christian worship is, in Samuel Terrien's phase, the liturgy of the Word that pervades the Scriptures and is incarnate in the living Christ. And what Christ is

131

by nature, his Body the church is by grace, particularly in its worship, where his Spirit flourishes.

Third, if this is true, then the good estate of both Scripture and worship are inseparably linked at every level. The bad estate of either not only weakens the other but may well put the very life of the Word at risk. Scripture without continual canonical enactment, by which the Word pervading it can be newly heard and appropriated by those to whom it is directed, becomes a knot of merely literary problems — a collection of ancient stories among whose moral lessons one may pick and choose. Liturgical worship without the scriptural Word is eyeless in Gaza, no longer able to discern the incarnate Word still living in the midst of the worshiping community, which becomes brittle and bored, at best succumbing to the latest forms of works of righteousness.

To receive the Word of God, therefore, is not like receiving a telephone call, not like getting an idea. The Word of God is always a revelation; we stand before it always like Moses before the mystery of a burning bush, in awe, reverence — worshipfully. As fallen creatures, there is no other way to stand in the divine presence.

Perhaps by now you can sense my thesis. It is that if the Bible needs reclaiming in the church (I doubt that anyone can reclaim it *for* the church) it must follow necessarily that the church's worship must be reclaimed as well. To push the thesis farther, I suggest that liturgical dysfunction may well be a major reason for biblical dysfunction in the church. As I see it, this situation has two roots, neither of which has received much commentary in the literature.

One root is in the hermeneutic employed in medieval explanations of the liturgy. As practiced by its first major proponent in the West, Amalarius of Metz, during the Carolingian renaissance of the ninth century, this sort of liturgical explanation sought to commend the old pre-medieval Roman liturgical usage — to "inculturate" it, so to speak — among the Teutonic tribes still being converted and civilized from Seville to Aachen. The Gallican and Visigothic liturgical systems that these tribes had generated some four centuries earlier were rapidly giving way to hybridizations of the immensely prestigious usages of Rome, fostered less by the papacy than by Charlemagne for the political unification of the infant Western empire.

A major problem in commending old Roman liturgical usage was its symbolic, spiritual, and ceremonial austerity. This made it about as accessible to the Teutonic mind-set as the British parliamentary system is to postcolonial India. The old Roman liturgy was in black and white; Teutonic liturgies were in technicolor, resembling nothing if not the title page of the *Book of Kells* — colorful, complex, and outlandishly flamboyant. Amalarius had no choice but to commend Roman worship forms by explaining them to an alien mind-set that found imagination in quantity to be irresistible.

Understandable in its purpose, Amalarius's explanation of the liturgy unwittingly laid down a repertoire of fancifully assigned meanings for every aspect of liturgical behavior, which was added to by subsequent commentators including Durandus of Mende in the late thirteenth century, who gave final form to the medieval liturgy by now riddled (as was biblical exegesis) with allegory. This hermeneutic was rapidly collapsing by the sixteenth century under pressure from intellectual shifts we today call "the Renaissance." Thomas More of England summed up the reaction of his time when he criticized an allegorical sermon he sat through at Oxford in the company of Henry VIII as "about as useful as milking a he-goat into a sieve." Liturgically, what had begun seven hundred years before in assigning allegorical meaning to liturgical ceremonies was ending in the creation of ceremonies meant to support this or that allegory, an endeavor that brought liturgy into disrepute for Renaissance minds.

This explains the Reformers' special hostility not only toward liturgy of this sort, but toward liturgy itself. It also accounts for the urge of many Catholics to replace allegorical meaning in the liturgy with orthodox theological meanings, a move that emphasized the liturgy as a form of education and deemphasized liturgy as an act of worship, and views the church as an educational rather than a worshiping community. Receiving the Word of God must then be understood as an educational rather than a worshipful act. This fatally relativized the unique authority of Scripture, making it one "source" among other educational "sources."

But the hunt for liturgical meanings intensifies liturgical dysfunction even more. If, for example, there are two candles on the altar *because* there are two natures in Christ (a theological allegory heard even in our own day), one can sense how "meaning" will tend to dissolve form. For if two candles will get the meaning across, then any candles will do, even the cheapest. What is generated is kitsch, in which modern liturgy is often awash, a situation that contributes once again to liturgical disrepute and dysfunction. One more opportunity for our race to experience the worshipful glory of God in his holy Word is smothered by a "pot of message." The church's income from this stupid little investment is meager indeed.

The other root of modern liturgical dysfunction is related to the first but is of later origin. It is the technological breakthrough resulting in the fifteenth-century invention of moveable type by Gutenberg. It is estimated that between 1450 and 1500 the new European presses published thirty thousand editions and some 10 million books, as against only fifty thousand manuscripts produced from scriptoria during the entire century. This explosion in the dissemination of knowledge, unequaled until our time, focused Western imagination on texts, made texts easily and cheaply changeable for the first time, put their fate in the hands of committees of experts that were quickly organized into centralized bureaucracies, and thus gave rise to the modern state. It also put liturgical texts for the first time into the hands of anyone who wanted them: The words formerly only heard in a ritual setting, a public enactment, could now be seen, retrieved, mulled over, diagrammed, changed from year to year or in even less time. The texts, moreover, could be shorn of their ritual setting and debated by the extrinsically certified. Immovable pews, unknown before the sixteenth century, became necessary in order to handle an increasing number of worship materials for the laity. Pews nailed the people down, causing congregations to resemble, for the first time ever, an audience attending a performance. The chasm between clergy and laity was thus widened, to the point of reducing the status of the baptized laity and making clergy seem to be, visibly and repeatedly, what in our own day has come to the called "first-class citizens" in the church — a status that cannot in justice be denied to anyone else.

The liturgical disenfranchisement of the laity was, of course, easily translatable into political terms that have fueled every Western revolutionary movement of the eighteenth through the twentieth centuries — movements that resist not only established order and any manifestation of authority as "elitist," but any order and authority at all. Indeed, society itself, with its inevitable orders of due process based on one form of authority or another, is increasingly seen as the "Great Oppressor," victimizing its members necessarily.

The ability to alter liturgy rapidly, radically, and in quantity was made possible by the invention of printing to a degree that the slow and laborious production of manuscripts could not match. Inherent in printing as applied to liturgical reform have been the unavoidable effects of relativizing the authority of Christian worship, of demoralizing the Christian community, and of loosening the social bond to the extent that liturgical acts become less public acts of unity in faith than skirmishes between ideological special-interest groups. The liturgy is again brought into disrepute; the Word of God is no longer received worshipfully and heard as the revelation it is.

The modern liberal mind is fabricated from these influences, and Christians are not immune to them. They pervade our assumptions and discourse. They are distilled and concentrated by the print and electronic media. They are, often unwittingly, one suspects, disseminated and canonized in many of our academic institutions, fed with little resistance to students, and said in Christian quarters to be the academy's service to the churches. It is difficult for me to see how, when the reciprocal authorities of Bible and worship collapse, the church can maintain its own unique identity, much less be taken seriously in the public square.

If we wish to reverse this lethal situation, a good place to start might be to restore the Bible to the church by first restoring the church's worship, for it is here that God's Word is meant to be received in what is neither more nor less than the liturgy of that same Word, both written and received. Here is where the Word takes on lively form in our midst. Separated from it, the Word falls on stony ground indeed.

We must understand anew that neither Word nor liturgy is about meanings, not even pious and exalted meanings. They are manifestations of reality — like a great mountain or a head of lettuce. We may derive meanings from them, but given our fallen nature it would be wise to derive these meanings with the greatest caution lest we miss the real and ingest our own lethal fabrications. This is, I think, why both Scripture and liturgy are "canonical," that is, so crucial are they for the life of the world that we deploy and enact them according to rules made by the wisdom of generations of those who have loved God by no criterion other than his grace. Small messages from special interest groups regularly fail in this; more often, they blind and deafen us to the awful transcendent reality of God in Christ in whose presence it is necessary for us to stand in order to remain faithful.

I do not think that a few verses of a severely edited psalm, a hymn or two, a brief sentence of Scripture for a preacher to muse on, and a sensitive "pastoral prayer" will be enough to reclaim the Bible and the liturgy for the church in its divine mission. The liturgy must be awash in Scripture, the divine presence must be worshiped in the beauty of holiness, the Word celebrated and declaimed above and beyond the limits of human politics and therapy. This fallen world of our own making must be able to come here at all times to see what we are really up to, and then we must have the courage to take the consequences, if necessary in our own flesh. Compromise this, and there is nothing left but kitsch, Bible stories, and endless talk about theological education for the overeducated.

We must also learn that enfranchising the entire faithful assembly is what holy baptism, not ordination, is about. A baptized community is never a passive community of the merely led. It is the Body of Christ, the corporate presence still on this earth of him in whom dwells the fullness of the Godhead bodily — a royal priesthood, a holy nation. Passive congregations confined to immovable pews while ordained experts (who sometimes confuse seminary theology with faith) work them over belie all this. We must recover baptism, its practice and piety, to free the church to receive God's Word in the beauty of holiness.

These realizations on our part are, of course, not all that needs to be done to reclaim biblical and liturgical authority in the church, but they are a good start. No one will do it for us because only we, the church as a whole, can do it — not for ourselves, but for the life of the world. And as we do it under grace and promise, I haven't the slightest doubt that our mutual schisms, which seem so daunting when we regard them singly and up close, will vanish, for instead of being mere denominations, each pushing its own claims, we shall have rediscovered how to be the church, Christ's bride and lover.